Museum & Art Gallery Graphics

Museum & Art Gallery Graphics

Edited by Wei Yew

Published by Quon Editions
© 1993

Printed in Canada by
Quality Color Press

First Edition 1993

Quon Editions
#203, 10107 – 115 Street
Edmonton, Alberta
T5K 1T3 Canada

Museum and Art Gallery Graphics

Includes bibliographical references and index.

ISBN 0-9696831-0-3

1. Art publicity – Pictorial works. 2. Public relations –
Museums – Pictorial works. 3. Advertising – Art
museums – Pictorial works. 4. Advertising –Museums –
Pictorial works. 5. Graphic arts. I. Yew, Wei, 1943 – .

NC998.4.M88 1993   741.6'7   C93-090148-7

Museum & Art Gallery Graphics

Edited by Wei Yew

Quon Editions

Design & Production
Studio 3 Graphics
Colour Separations
BK Trade Colour, Canada
Printer
Quality Color Press, Canada

Contents

To the many artists, curators and designers who have shared their talents in this book.

Special thanks to:

All the museums and art galleries who have sent a wealth of material for this book,

Mary Yeow

Sheila Laughton

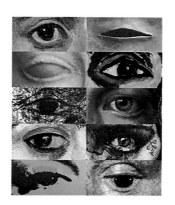

The works reproduced in *Museum & Art Gallery Graphics* represent an impressive as well as extensive range of graphic material designed for museums & art galleries from many countries including Australia, England, Mexico, Canada and the United States.

Graphics programs from 18 institutions are dealt with in depth beginning with the signage system of the Victoria and Albert Museum in England. Other signage systems represented are those of the Musée des Beaux-Arts de Montréal, British Museum of Modern Art, the Tate Galleries, the American Museum of Natural History and the Smithsonian Washington Mall. Of particular interest is the Museo de Arte Contemporáneo which employs a signage theme based on the pre-Hispanic stone rings found in ball courts. Also noteworthy from these featured institutions are their promotional campaigns, exhibits, exhibition posters, invitations and catalogues.

Exhibition posters are perhaps the most visible graphic material produced by museums and art galleries. Here you will find a large section on brilliantly designed posters including the much-admired Mobil series designed by the firm of Chermayeff & Geismar Inc.

There is also an unforgettable section on print material covering the many creative brochures, invitations, gift bags, press ads, newsletters, catalogues and books designed for museums and art galleries around the world.

Wei Yew

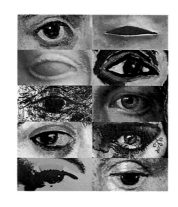

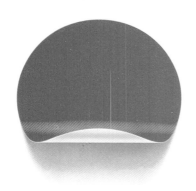

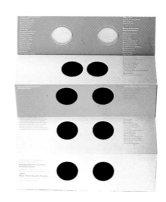

The Victoria and Albert is Britain's national museum of applied art and design and houses the finest collection of its kind. The building itself has been added to many times since its opening in 1852 and is a complex maze of galleries and architectural styles. The Trustees approached Pentagram to design a sign system which would guide visitors through this often confusing building.

Designers
Alan Fletcher, Quentin Newark
Design Firm
Pentagram Design Limited,
London, England
Client
Victoria & Albert Museum

The logotype for the museum uses the orignal 18th century typeface of Giambattista Bodoni. The design utilises the ampersand to replace the cross bar of the 'A', which invests the mark with its distinctive personality.

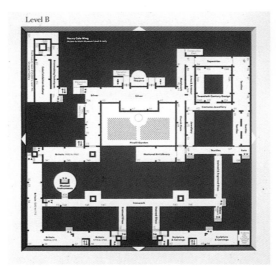

Level B

Pentagram's solution lay in a colour compass; red for north, green for south, blue for west and yellow for east. Colour-coded fabric banners suspended at the entrance to each gallery carry the name of the exhibition(s) in a typeface designed in the 18th century by Giambattista Bodoni. These link with a colour-coded map given to visitors when they enter the museum. Together the map and banners show visitors where they are and in which direction they are going.

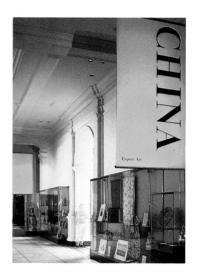

In 1988, The Montreal Museum of Fine Arts and its agency FOUG, adopted a "blockbuster strategy". Each exhibition was advertised and promoted as an event – a departure from the museum's practice of general corporate advertising. The result is a rich and varied body of work – generally produced from very limited budget – that has consistently raised the museum's profile over the past four years, and won a host of international honours.

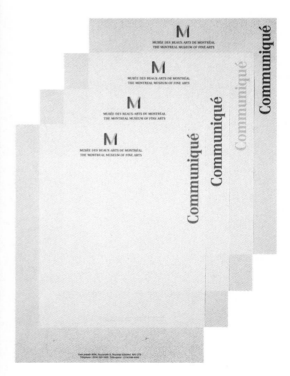

Signage

Creative/Art Director
Jean Morin
Designers
Alain Rochon - Identity
Pierre Lessard, Guy Dubuc,
Pierre Sasseville - Signage
Design Firm
Axion Inc., Montreal, Canada
Client
The Montreal Museum of Fine
Arts

Art Director/Designer
Pierre Drouin
Design Firm
FOUG, Montreal, Canada
Illustrator
Pierre Drouin
Photographers
Studio Aventure, Pierre Drouin

Gift bags

Gift sticker

MUSÉE DES BEAUX-ARTS
DE MONTRÉAL

Creative Director
Pierre Audet
Art Director/Designer
Pierre Drouin
Design Firm
FOUG, Montreal, Canada
Copywriters
Michel Lopez, Dianna Carr

THE ONLY GIFT
THAT COSTS MORE
AFTER CHRISTMAS.

This Christmas,
give a Friends of the Museum Card.
In the time it takes to make a phone call,
you can offer someone a whole new world.

The card gives the bearer unlimited access to all Museum
exhibitions. All year long. And with the opening of the Museum's
new wing, the privileges have nearly doubled!

But on January 1, 1992, the price of the card will nearly double,
too. So buy the card now. And make someone a Friend
for Christmas!

Adults: $30. Families: $45. Students and Seniors: $15. GST extra.
Call 285-1600.

THE MONTREAL MUSEUM
OF FINE ARTS

Print ad

L'ARCHITECTVRE DE EDWARD & W.S. MAXWELL

13 DÉCEMBRE 1991-22 MARS 1992

M MUSÉE DES BEAUX-ARTS
DE MONTRÉAL

Les collectionneurs montréalais
1880-1920

MUSÉE DES BEAUX-ARTS DE MONTRÉAL
8 DÉCEMBRE 1989 - 25 FÉVRIER 1990

Creative Director
Pierre Audet
Art Director/Designer
Pierre Drouin
Design Firm
FOUG, Montreal, Canada
Illustrator
Maxwell
Copywriter
Michel Lopez

Exhibition poster

Ouvert sur la ville

Expositions 1992

Floor Plan

M MUSÉE DES BEAUX-ARTS
DE MONTRÉAL

Creative Director
Pierre Audet
Art Director/Designer
Nicole Labelle
Design Firm
FOUG, Montreal, Canada
Illustrator
Tissot
Copywriter
Normand Cayouette

Exhibition poster

Creative Director
Pierre Audet
Art Director/Designer
Pierre Drouin
Design Firm
FOUG, Montreal, Canada
Copywriter
Michel Lopez

Brochures

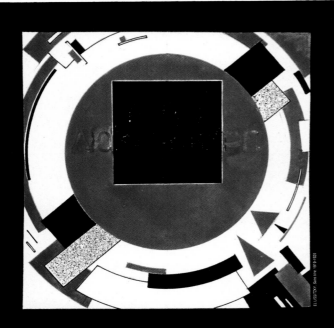

Creative Director
Pierre Audet
Art Director/Designer
Pierre Drouin
Design Firm
FOUG, Montreal, Canada
Copywriter
Michel Lopez

Exhibition posters

Page 17
Creative Director
Pierre Audet
Creative/Art Director
Pierre Drouin
Design Firm
FOUG, Montreal, Canada
Illustrator
Tamara de Lempicka
Copywriter
Michel Lopez

Exhibition banner

Creative Director
Pierre Audet
Art Director/Designer
Pierre Drouin
Design Firm
FOUG, Montreal, Canada
Illustrator
Jasper Johns
Copywriter
Michel Lopez

Exhibition poster

Jasper JOHNS. *Cible aux quatre faces*, 1979. Collection Walker Art Center, Minneapolis. ©Jasper Johns 1990/Vis*Art Droits d'auteur Inc.

JASPER JOHNS
S Y M B O L E S · I M P R E S S I O N S
MUSÉE DES BEAUX-ARTS DE MONTRÉAL · 14 DÉCEMBRE 1990 · 10 MARS 1991

MONET
ET LES IMPRESSIONNISTES

... suite
au Musée

UN REGARD PASSIONNÉ :
CHEFS-D'ŒUVRE DE L'IMPRESSIONNISME ET AUTRES TOILES DE MAÎTRES DE LA COLLECTION E.G. BUHRLE

MUSÉE DES BEAUX-ARTS DE MONTRÉAL
3 AOÛT - 14 OCTOBRE 1990

DEGAS
ET LES IMPRESSIONNISTES

... suite
au Musée

UN REGARD PASSIONNÉ :
CHEFS-D'ŒUVRE DE L'IMPRESSIONNISME ET AUTRES TOILES DE MAÎTRES DE LA COLLECTION E.G. BUHRLE

MUSÉE DES BEAUX-ARTS DE MONTRÉAL
3 AOÛT - 14 OCTOBRE 1990

ALFRED LALIBERTÉ

88 sculptures
MUSÉE DES BEAUX-ARTS
DE MONTRÉAL
23 mars - 20 mai 1990

CHASSEUR DE TÊTES

Creative Director
Pierre Audet
Art Director/Designer
Pierre Drouin
Design Firm
FOUG, Montreal, Canada
Copywriter
Michel Lopez

Exhibition posters

Creative Director
Pierre Audet
Art Director/Designer
Nicole Labelle
Design Firm
FOUG, Montreal, Canada
Photographer
Studio Ose
Copywriter
Normand Cayouette

Exhibition poster

MUSÉE DES BEAUX-ARTS   THE MONTREAL MUSEUM
DE MONTRÉAL   OF FINE ARTS

Creative Director
Pierre Audet
Art Director/Designer
Pierre Drouin
Design Firm
FOUG, Montreal, Canada
Illustrator
Riopelle
Copywriters
Michel Lopez, Dianna Carr

Exhibition posters and print ad

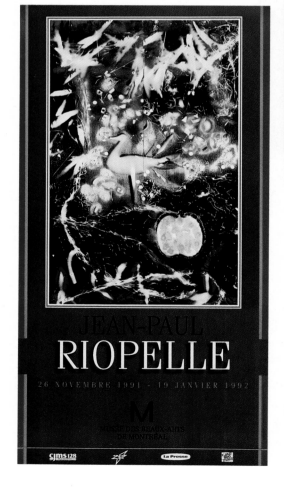

NOVEMBER 26, 1991 - JANUARY 19, 1992
FREE PASS

entitling you to visit the exhibition
on the day and at the time of your choice.
Open Tuesday to Sunday from 11 a.m. to 6 p.m.,
until 9 p.m. on Saturday.

THE MONTREAL MUSEUM
OF FINE ARTS
1380, Sherbrooke Street West
(514) 285-2000

36 heures pour dénouer l'Énigme des chefs-d'œuvre

Les Arts du Maurier Ltée

Le Musée ouvre sa nouvelle aile pendant 36 heures.

Du samedi 30 novembre à 10 h au dimanche 1er décembre à 22 h.

Venez dénouer l'Énigme des chefs-d'œuvre.
Un jeu palpitant qui pourrait vous faire gagner
un voyage pour deux en Martinique,
en Hollande ou en Tchécoslovaquie.
Ou l'un de nos 12 baladeurs Sharp.
Règlements disponibles au Musée des beaux-arts de Montréal

M MUSÉE DES BEAUX-ARTS DE MONTRÉAL

du Maurier Arts Ltd. presents:
Masterpiece Mystery
C O N T E S T

M
THE MONTREAL MUSEUM OF FINE ARTS

Track down 3 masterpieces and you could win a trip for two to Martinique, Czechoslovakia or Holland, or one of 12 Sharp personal stereo cassette players!

Here's how to play:
- On this "Masterpiece Map" are six elements of six different paintings. Follow the visual and written clues. They'll lead you to the masterpieces! (First clue: they're all in the new wing, the Jean-Noël Desmarais Pavilion!)
- You must identify three of the six paintings, and write their titles on the entry form included. Deposit it in the Masterpiece Mystery Contest box on the main floor.
- Winners' names will be drawn December 1, 1991 at 10:30 p.m. Good luck!

1.
Brueghel got cold feet painting this couple going home in the snow.
Permanent Collection, Level 4

2.
Sawatski painted a travel picture of a family hitched up to a lone prairie.
Carrefour, Level 1

3.
Painter Alex Colville knows that when the horse has bolted, it's too late to close the gate.
Contemporary Art, Level S2

4.
Was the woman in white pleased with her portrait? Only painter G.B. Tiepolo knows for sure.
Permanent Collection, Level 4

5.
She turned her back on a tropical paradise, and Henri Matisse captured it on canvas.
20ᵉ Century Art, Level 3

6.
Painter James Tissot thought her as splendidly beautiful as fall foliage.
Permanent Collection, Level 4

Masterpiece Mystery
C O N T E S T

The titles of the three paintings I have identified are:
1. _____
2. _____
3. _____

Name _____
Address _____

Postal Code _____
Telephone _____

Complete contest rules available at
The Montreal Museum of Fine Arts,
Post Office Box 3000, Station H, Montréal, Québec, H3G 2T9
Contest ends Sunday, December 1 at 10 p.m.
Draw to be held December 1, 1991 at 10:30 p.m.

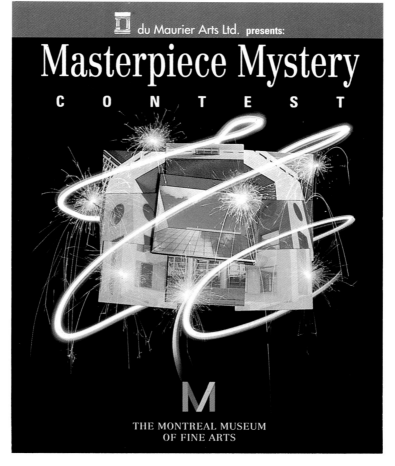

du Maurier Arts Ltd. presents:
Masterpiece Mystery
C O N T E S T

M
THE MONTREAL MUSEUM OF FINE ARTS

Creative Director
Pierre Audet
Art Director/Designer
Francis Tremblay
Design Firm
FOUG, Montreal, Canada
Photographer
Studio Aventure
Copywriters
Michel Lopez, Dianna Carr

Event print material

Creative Director
Pierre Audet
Art Director/Designer
Pierre Drouin
Design Firm
FOUG, Montreal, Canada
Photographer
Michael Batchelor
Copywriter
Michel Lopez

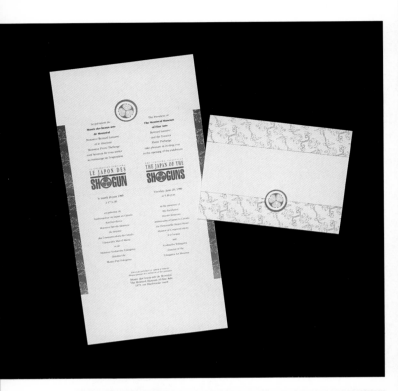

*Exhibition invitation,
brochure and poster*

Creative Director
Pierre Audet
Art Director/Designer
Pierre Drouin
Design Firm
FOUG, Montreal, Canada
Photographer
Studio Aventure
Copywriter
Michel Lopez

Poster

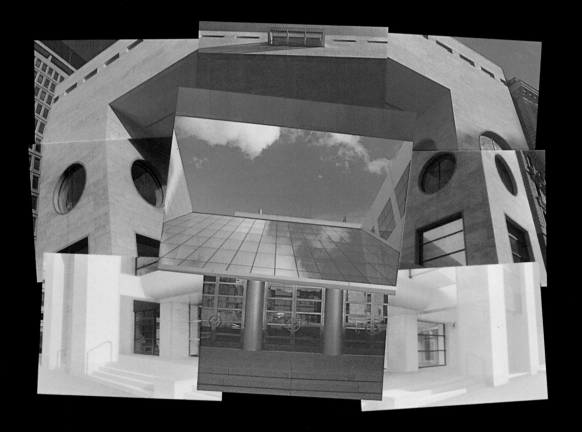

Creative Director
Pierre Audet
Art Director/Designer
Pierre Drouin
Design Firm
FOUG, Montréal, Canada
Photographer
André Cornellier
Illustrator
Bernard Leduc
Copywriters
Michel Lopez, Dianna Carr
Fabricator
Décor 3D

Exhibition promotional material

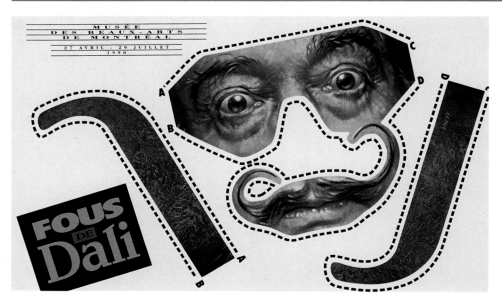

5

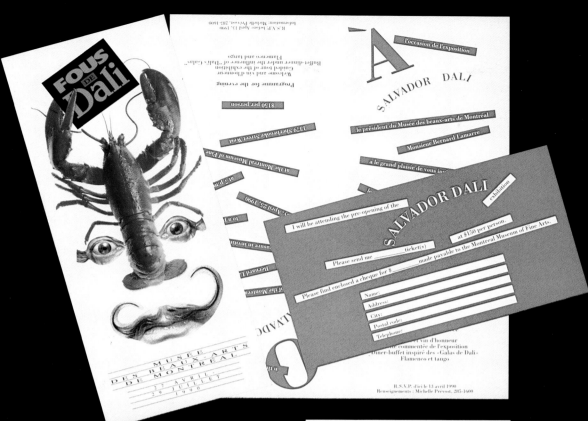

PICK A CARD.
A FRIENDS OF THE
MUSEUM CARD.

Adults: $30, Family: $45
Students and Seniors: $15

DALIBOLICAL DEAL!

With the card, here's what you get:

Mad for Dali April 27 to July 29
The Impressionists August 3 to October 14
Every other exhibition for a full year!

Without the card,
Dali and the Impressionists will cost you $20.
Spend $10 more, and see it all!
(Credit cards accepted: Visa, Mastercard, Amex)

YOU'D BE MAD
TO MISS IT!
(514) 285-1600

THE
MONTREAL MUSEUM
OF FINE ARTS

For over a year the Crafts Council was threatened with reduced funding and a take-over by the more powerful Arts Council. When the organization won its right to independence through parliament, a new identity was used to re-launch the society and confirm its status as representative of the crafts professions.

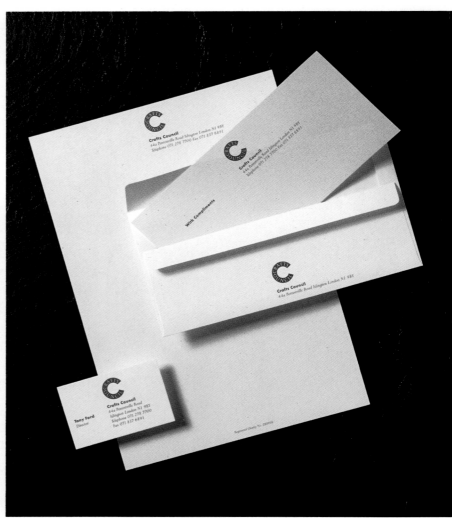

Pentagram's design for the identity uses craft to convey the message; the lettering of the logotype is by Tom Perkins, a letter cutter on the Council's Index of Selected Makers, a listing of 500 leading craftspeople in Britain.

Designers
John Rushworth, Vince Frost
Design Firm
Pentagram Design Limited,
London, England
Client
Crafts Council

Signage and gift bag

**Beyond the
Dovetail**
An exhibition of
skill and imagination
in many crafts

19 September –10 November

New address
Crafts Council
44a Pentonville Road
Islington London N1 9BY
Telephone 071 278 7700

Free admission
Open Tuesday to Saturday 11am–6pm
Sunday 2–6pm Closed Monday

2 minutes from Angel tube

**Beyond The
Dovetail**
Craft, Skill and
Imagination

Edited by Christopher Frayling

Mingei
The living tradition in Japanese arts

An exhibition of works from the Japan Folk Crafts Museum
21 November - 12 January

Sponsored in London by Sanwa Bank
in Japan by Fuji Xerox, Dai Nippon Printing Company,
Security Communication and Nippon Telegraph and Telephone Corporation.
British tour organised by Glasgow Museums.
Designed by Pentagram

Free admission
Open Tuesday to Saturday 11am - 6pm
Sunday 2 - 6pm Closed Monday
Christmas opening
Normal hours, except closed on
December 25, 26, 27. Open New Year's Day.

New address
Crafts Council Gallery
44a Pentonville Road
Islington London N1 9BY
Telephone 071 278 7700
2 minutes from Angel tube

Annual report

Poster

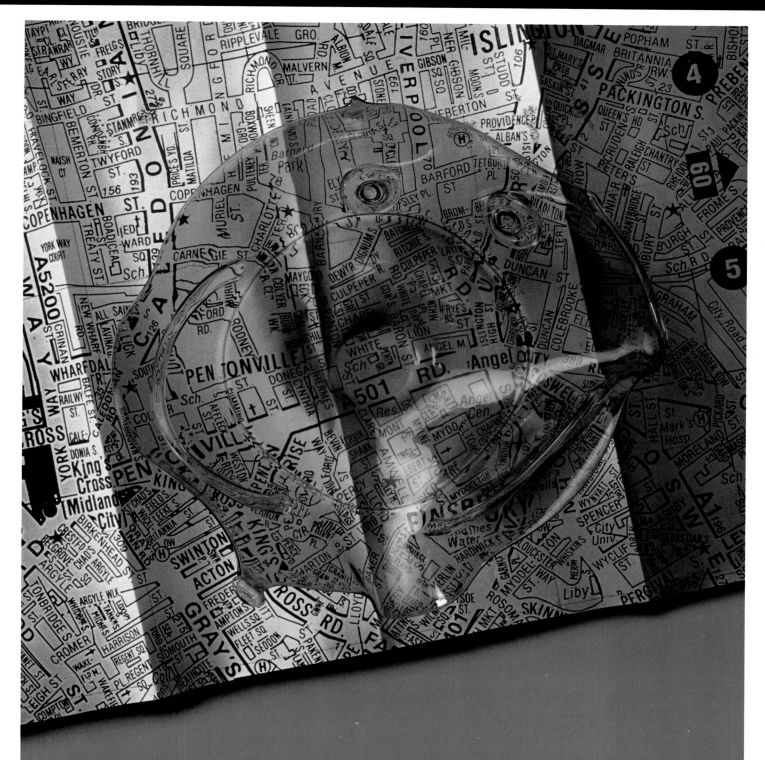

Open from 19 September 1991
The new national centre for the crafts

Admission free
Open Tuesdays to Saturdays 11am-6pm
Sundays 2-6pm Closed Mondays

Crafts Council
44a Pentonville Road
Islington London N1 9BY
Telephone 071 278 7700

2 minutes from Angel tube

Crafts Council
Gallery, Collection,
Information, Library,
Educational workshop,
Shop and Café

Best known for its wealth of French Impressionist paintings, The Art Institute of Chicago is one of America's preeminent art museums. Its collections encompass over forty centuries of art from Africa, the Americas, Asia, and Europe. Approximately 260,000 works are held in ten curatorial departments. Particularly strong are holdings in Japanese prints, Chinese ceramics, 18th and 19th century French drawings, photography, 20th century art from Europe and America, and architectural drawings.

Art Director/Designer
Ann Wassmann Gross
Design Firm & Client
The Art Institute of Chicago, Illinois

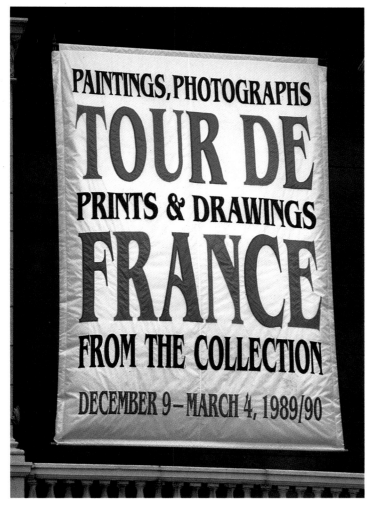

Exhibition posters

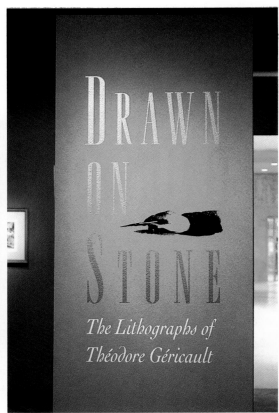

Art Director/Designer
Ann Wassmann Gross
Design Firm & Client
The Art Institute of Chicago,
Illinois

The design program of Papalote, the Children's Museum of México City which is scheduled to open in 1993, includes the museum logo, an icon for each of the five exhibit areas, service symbols, and a system of signs, maps, and print materials. The museum logo is a butterfly-kite. The name "Papalote" means kite in Spanish, and the word "Papálotl" means butterfly in the Aztec Nahuatl language. The geometric forms in the wings of the logo suggest the museum's geometric buildings designed by architect Ricardo Legorreta.

Calling card

A fold-out annual report based on the pre-Hispanic Codex format

The kite represents an interactive toy, common to all México children.

Entrance sculpture

Art Director/Designer
Lance Wyman
Designers
Denise Guerra, Linda Iskander
Design Firm
Lance Wyman Ltd., New York
Architect
Ricardo Legorreta, México City-
Los Angeles

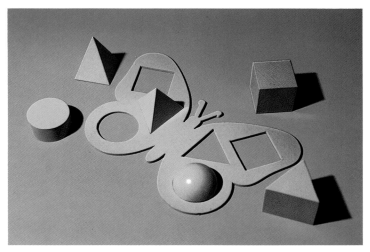

Logo geometric study

Studies of directional signs

Icon stack – icons for each of the exhibit areas

The Museum of Modern Art, Oxford is housed in a converted Victorian brewery and exhibits international contemporary art.

The architecture of the building, with its metal columns and structured layout, inspired the linear pattern of the new identity, while an extra black modern typeface provided dramatic contrast for the name. The approach was carried through to a sign system for the building.

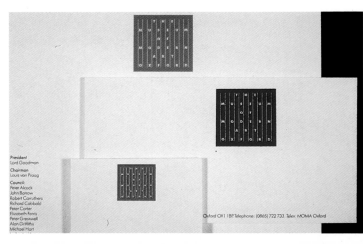

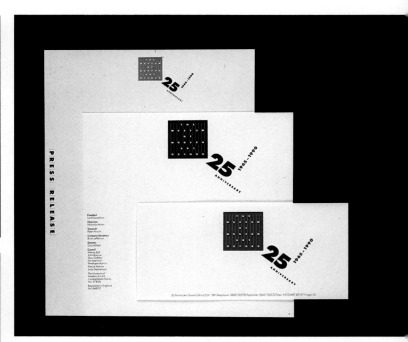

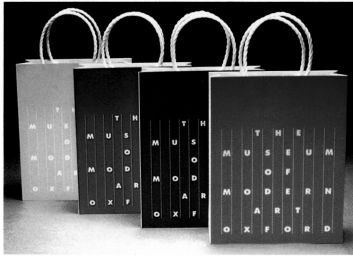

Designers
Mervyn Kurlansky, Robert Dunnet
Design Firm
Pentagram Design Limited, London, England
Client
Museum of Modern Art, Oxford

Stationery

Gift bags

Exterior signage

The architectural detailing of the building with its grid layout and cast iron columns inspired the fine linear pattern of the designs, while contrasting bold san serif letters provided a strong contemporary look. The same graphic approach was carried through to banners, posters and promotional items to be sold in the museum shop.

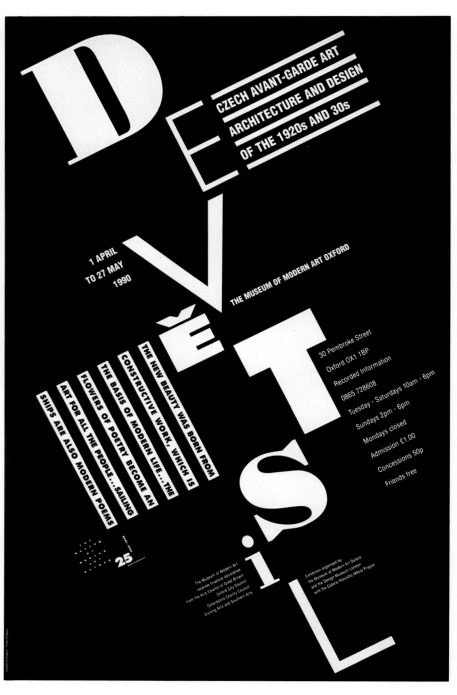

Exhibition posters

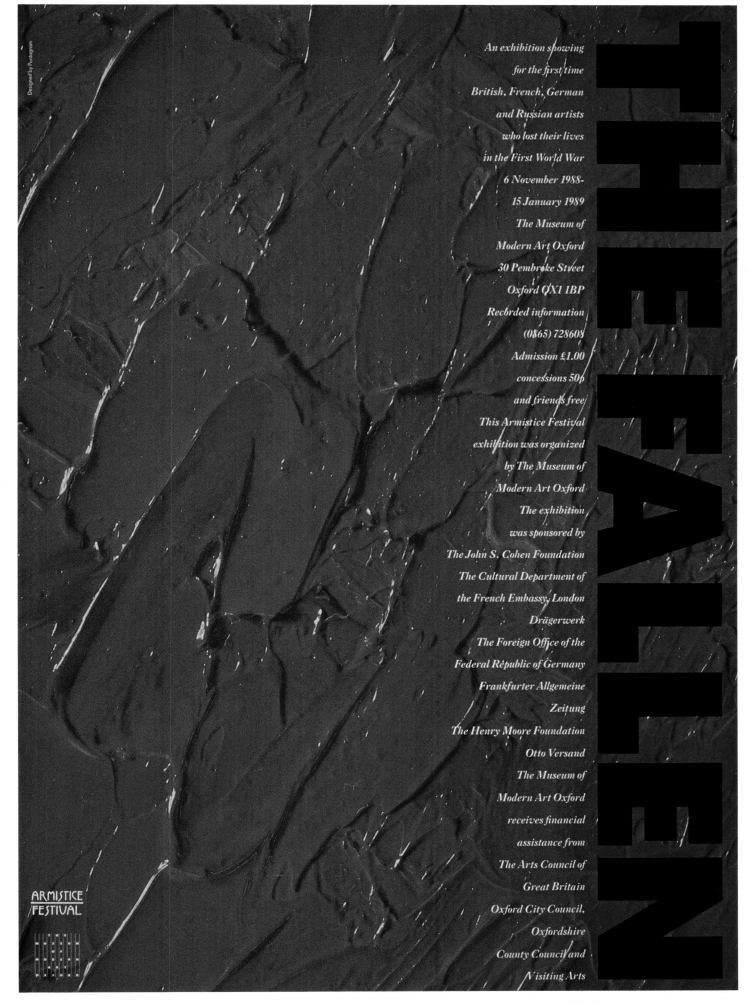

THE FALLEN

An exhibition showing
for the first time
British, French, German
and Russian artists
who lost their lives
in the First World War
6 November 1988-
15 January 1989
The Museum of
Modern Art Oxford
30 Pembroke Street
Oxford OX1 1BP
Recorded information
(0865) 728608
Admission £1.00
concessions 50p
and friends free
This Armistice Festival
exhibition was organized
by The Museum of
Modern Art Oxford
The exhibition
was sponsored by
The John S. Cohen Foundation
The Cultural Department of
the French Embassy, London
Drägerwerk
The Foreign Office of the
Federal Republic of Germany
Frankfurter Allgemeine
Zeitung
The Henry Moore Foundation
Otto Versand
The Museum of
Modern Art Oxford
receives financial
assistance from
The Arts Council of
Great Britain
Oxford City Council,
Oxfordshire
County Council and
Visiting Arts

Designed by Pentagram

ARMISTICE
FESTIVAL

Exhibition poster

Exhibition poster

**HELEN CHADWICK:
VIRAL LANDSCAPES**

5 NOVEMBER 1989 – 7 JANUARY 1990

THE MUSEUM OF MODERN ART OXFORD

The Museum of Modern Art receives financial assistance from The Arts Council of Great Britain, Oxford City Council, Oxfordshire County Council, Visiting Arts, and Southern Arts. Perspex sponsor Talbot Designs Limited

Detail from Viral Landscape No.3 1988-1989 etched on Crosfield computer system

30 Pembroke St. Oxford OX1 1BP

Recorded Information: 0865 728608

Admission £1.00 Concessions 50p Friends Free

Tuesdays – Saturdays 10am - 6pm Sundays 2am - 6pm Mondays Closed

Exhibition poster

SOUL BURNING FLASHES

YAYOI KUSAMA: SCULPTURE

5 NOVEMBER 1989 – 7 JANUARY 1990

THE MUSEUM OF MODERN ART OXFORD

With financial assistance from The Japan Foundation. The Museum of Modern Art receives financial assistance from The Arts Council of Great Britain, Oxford City Council, Oxfordshire County Council, Visiting Arts, and Southern Arts

30 Pembroke St. Oxford OX1 1BP

Recorded Information: 0865 728608

Admission £1.00 Concessions 50p Friends Free

Tuesdays – Saturdays 10am - 6pm Sundays 2am - 6pm Mondays Closed

Exhibition poster

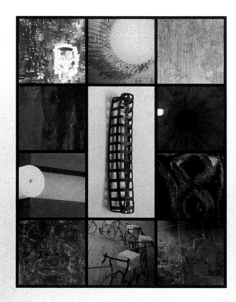

NORTHLANDS
NEW ART FROM SCANDINAVIA
14 JANUARY - 18 MARCH 1990

THE MUSEUM OF MODERN ART OXFORD

The Museum of Modern Art receives financial assistance from The Arts Council of Great Britain, Oxford City Council, Oxfordshire County Council, Visiting Arts, Organised by MOMA and the Nordic Arts Centre Helsinki

30 Pembroke St. Oxford OX1 1BP
Recorded Information: 0865 728608
Admission £1.00 Concessions 50p Friends Free
Tuesdays – Saturdays 10am – 6pm Sundays 2am – 6pm Mondays Closed

ART AT THE EDGE

Contemporary Art from Poland 18 September-30 October 1988. The Museum of Modern Art Oxford 30 Pembroke Street, Oxford OX1 1BP. Recorded information (0865) 728608. Admission £1.00, concessions 50p and friends free. The exhibition was organised by The Museum of Modern Art Oxford with The National Museum Wroclaw. The Museum of Modern Art Oxford receives financial assistance from the Arts Council of Great Britain, Oxford City Council, Oxfordshire County Council and Visiting Arts

Exhibition posters

SHIRAZEH HOUSHIARY: SCULPTURE 6 NOVEMBER 1988 – 15 JANUARY 1989
THE MUSEUM OF MODERN ART OXFORD 30 PEMBROKE STREET OXFORD OX1 1BP RECORDED INFORMATION (0865) 728608
ADMISSION £1.00, CONCESSIONS 50P AND FRIENDS FREE THE EXHIBITION WAS ORGANISED BY THE CENTRE
D'ART CONTEMPORAIN, GENEVA WITH THE MUSEUM OF MODERN ART OXFORD WITH THANKS TO THE LISSON
GALLERY LONDON, THE MUSEUM OF MODERN ART OXFORD RECEIVES FINANCIAL ASSISTANCE FROM
THE ARTS COUNCIL OF GREAT BRITAIN, OXFORD CITY COUNCIL, OXFORD COUNTY COUNCIL AND VISITING ARTS

To encourage buyer confidence, the gallery owners developed a program to guarantee the authenticity of the property they sold. To visually communicate the galleries who stood behind the guarantee, a symbol based on membership in the Place des Antiquaires Merchants Association was designed. This sticker was placed prominently on the entry door to the participating galleries

Art Director
Harriet Walley
Designer
Stacy Mannheim
Design Firm
Harriet Walley Associates,
New York
Bookbinder
Elena Laza
Copywriter
Harriet Walley
Client
Lowy

This invitation was designed to invite clients to an exhibition of antique frames dating from 1450 and to introduce them to a new location for the company. The clients included museum curators, international art dealers and collectors.

Art Director/Designer
Stacy Mannheim
Design Firm
Harriet Walley Associates,
New York
Illustrator/Photographer
Stacy Mannheim
Client
Place des Antiquaires Guarantee

Place des Antiquaires
The international center of art and antiques

More than 40 galleries specializing in antique European & American furniture, paintings & sculpture, Oriental works of art, antique and period jewelry, art nouveau, art deco, ceramics & glass, copper and brass, Russian works of art & icons, silver, books and manuscripts, autographs, maps, prints, dolls & automata, rugs & tapestries, pipes & canes, scientific and marine instruments, objects of vertu, gold boxes, ivories & fans

Open to the public Monday through Saturday 11am to 6pm
For information and a complete listing of our galleries, please call or write Place des Antiquaires
125 East 57th Street   New York, NY 10022   212.758.2900

Art Director
Harriet Walley
Designer
Marianne Matte
Design Firm
Harriet Walley Associates,
New York

Photographer
Josh Greene
Gene Moore - Stylist
Copywriter
Harriet Walley
Client
Place des Antiquaires

A series of advertisements to show at least one object from each of the galleries

The Imperial War Museum is the national museum of the 20th century war, recording all aspects of conflict, civilian and military. To coincide with the redevelopment of the museum, a new visual identity was commissioned. The symbol incorporates the initials WM in the form of searchlights against a background of land, sea and sky. This element is extended for use on murals and promotional material.

Design Firm
Minale, Tattersfield & Partners,
Surrey, England
Client
Imperial War Museum, London

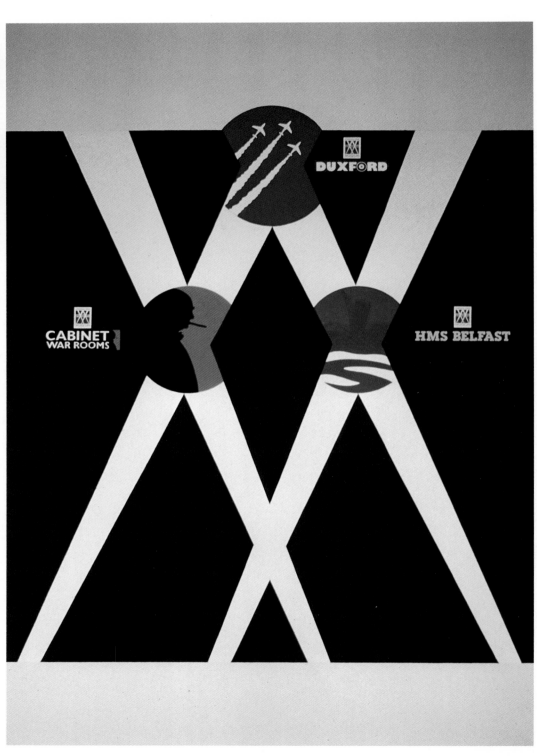

The Monterrey Museum of Contemporary Art (MARCO), designed by architect Ricardo Legoretta, opened in 1991. The visual identity and signage system for MARCO evolves from the design of the museum logo. The letter "O" is squared to suggest the museum's central patio and the name, MARCO, which means "frame" in Spanish. The squared "O" logo element is applied consistently to the museum's signage and

printed materials. Brochures, invitations, banners and signs are designed with a cut-through square center. The design of the museum's wall signposts is inspired by stone rings found in pre-Hispanic ball courts.

Art Director/Designer
Lance Wyman
Designers
Denise Guerra, Linda Iskander
Design Firm
Lance Wyman Ltd., New York
Architect
Ricardo Legorreta, México City-Los Angeles

*Wall signpost inspired by the
pre-Hispanic stone rings found in
ball courts*

Service symbols

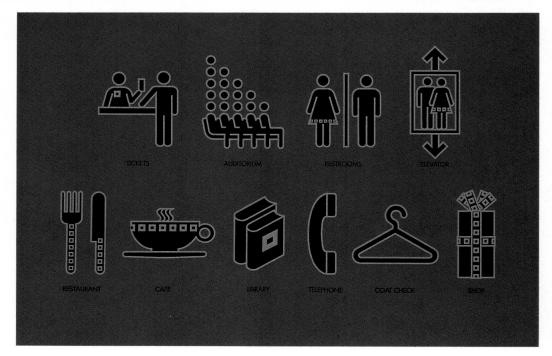

TICKETS   AUDITORIUM   RESTROOMS   ELEVATOR

RESTAURANT   CAFE   LIBRARY   TELEPHONE   COAT CHECK   SHOP

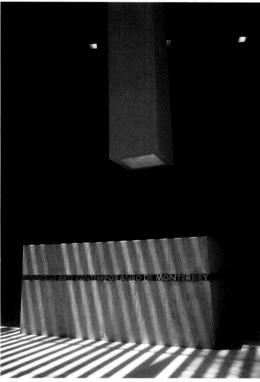

Exterior banners

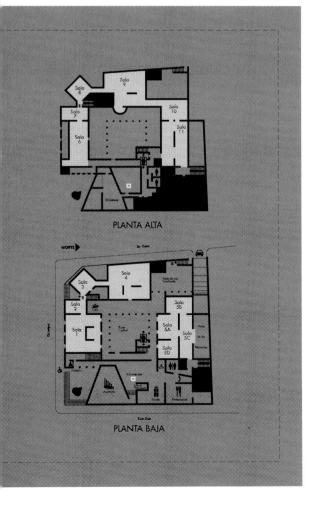

PLANTA ALTA

PLANTA BAJA

Diagrammatic maps

Die-cut invitation

Transparent bag

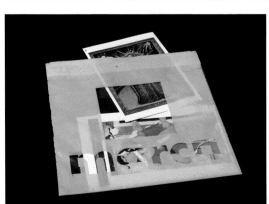

TATE
GALLERY

At the beginning of 1990, the new director of the Tate Gallery carried out the most extensive re-hang of the collection since the gallery's opening in 1887. Pentagram was commissioned to design a new sign system, information literature and identity.

The brief asked for a low-key, timeless logotype which would not compete with the art and would use a typeface specially cut for the gallery in the early '80s by type-designers Michael Harvey and Professor Herbert Spencer.

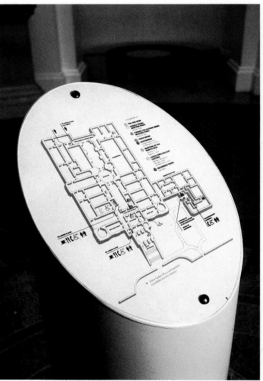

Designers
David Hillman, Jo Swindell
Design Firm
Pentagram Design Limited,
London, England
Client
Tate Gallery, London

Free-standing signs were designed to echo the columns of the Tate Gallery building and serve a variety of functions. With only slight modification they act as route and gallery indicators, leaflet dispensers, location maps and, occasionally, lecterns. They are produced in 'stone' and 'terracotta', and compliment the natural colours of their surroundings. Fixed wall-mounted signs carry text pertaining to particular galleries, and again are colour co-ordinated with the interiors.

The logotype appears on stationery, posters, catalogues and other promotional literature, usually in the Tate's house-colour red, or in grey.

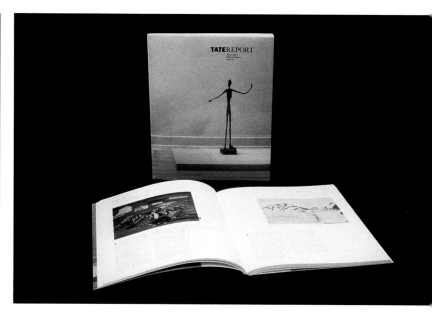

Events newsletter

Postcards

Annual report

Information kit

BLAKE
at the Tate

On display in the Collection
of the Tate Gallery

Admission free
Monday – Saturday 10 – 5.50
Sunday 2 – 5.50
Pimlico Underground (Victoria Line)
Tate Gallery, Millbank, London SW1
Recorded Information: 071-821 7128

TATE
GALLERY

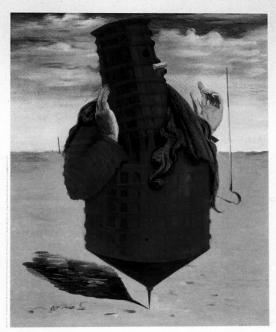

Max Ernst

13 February–21 April 1991
Monday–Saturday 10–5.50
Sunday 2–5.50 (Last admission 5.15)
Closed Good Friday, 29 March
Admission £4 Concessions £2
Pimlico Underground (Victoria Line)
Tate Gallery, Millbank, London SW1

Sponsored by
DAIMLERBENZ

TATE
GALLERY

Pop
Prints

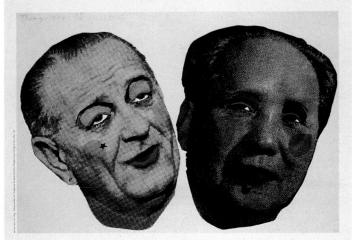

*Aspects of Printmaking in
Britain and the USA 1959–1982*
6 March–23 June 1991

Admission free
Monday–Saturday 10–5.50
Sunday 2–5.50
Closed Good Friday, 29 March
Pimlico Underground (Victoria Line)
Tate Gallery, Millbank, London SW1
Recorded Information: 071-821 7128

TATE
GALLERY

MONDRIAN
at the Tate

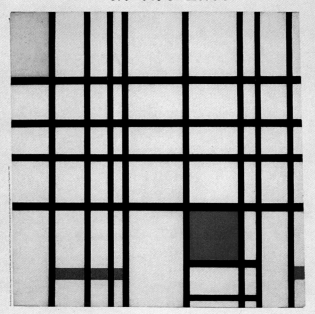

On display in the Collection
of the Tate Gallery

Admission free
Monday – Saturday 10 – 5.50
Sunday 2 – 5.50
Pimlico Underground (Victoria Line)
Tate Gallery, Millbank, London SW1
Recorded Information: 071-821 7128

TATE
GALLERY

An Exhibition of Work
by Shortlisted Artists

6 November–
8 December 1991

Sponsored by Channel 4

Tate Gallery, Millbank,
London SW1

**The Turner Prize
1991**

Ian Davenport
Anish Kapoor
Fiona Rae
Rachel Whiteread

TATE GALLERY | THE TURNER PRIZE 1991 | 4

Exhibition posters

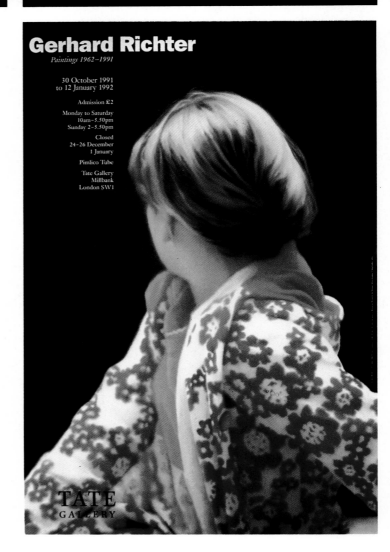

An Exhibition of Work
by Shortlisted Artists

6 November –
8 December 1991

Sponsored by Channel 4

Tate Gallery, Millbank,
London SW1

**The Turner Prize
1991**

Ian Davenport
Anish Kapoor
Fiona Rae
Rachel Whiteread

TATE | THE TURNER PRIZE 1991 | 4

ON CLASSIC GROUND

Picasso, Léger, de Chirico and the New Classicism, 1910–30

6 June – 2 September 1990

Monday – Saturday 10 – 5.50
Sunday 2 – 5.50 (last admission 5.15)
Admission £4 Concessions £2
Pimlico Underground (Victoria Line)
Tate Gallery, Millbank, London SW1

TATE
GALLERY

Sponsored by
REED INTERNATIONAL

ON CLASSIC GROUND

Picasso, Léger, de Chirico and
the New Classicism, 1910–30

6 June – 2 September 1990

Monday – Saturday 10 – 5.50
Sunday 2 – 5.50 (last admission 5.15)
Admission £4 Concessions £2
Pimlico Underground (Victoria Line)
Tate Gallery, Millbank, London SW1

TATE
GALLERY

Sponsored by
REED INTERNATIONAL

ON CLASSIC GROUND

Picasso, Léger, de Chirico and
the New Classicism, 1910–30

6 June – 2 September 1990

Monday – Saturday 10 – 5.50
Sunday 2 – 5.50 (last admission 5.15)
Admission £4 Concessions £2
Pimlico Underground (Victoria Line)
Tate Gallery, Millbank, London SW1

TATE
GALLERY

Sponsored by
REED INTERNATIONAL

LIST OF WORKS EXHIBITED

Ian Davenport
Born 1966

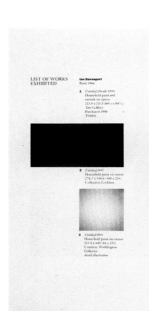

Anish Kapoor
Born 1954

Fiona Rae
Born 1963

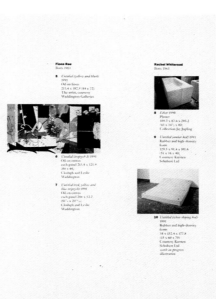

Rachel Whiteread
Born 1963

Exhibition catalogue

FIONA RAE

TATE GALLERY LIVERPOOL

The Tate Gallery is situated in the Albert Docks, as part of a new development in Liverpool. It is located in an old warehouse with a new interior that retains many of the building's original features.

Using the Tate Gallery's crest, in grey or embossed, combined with a simple Futura typeface in black, Pentagram's design expressed both the tradition of the Tate and the new thinking behind this first 'outstation' of the London gallery.

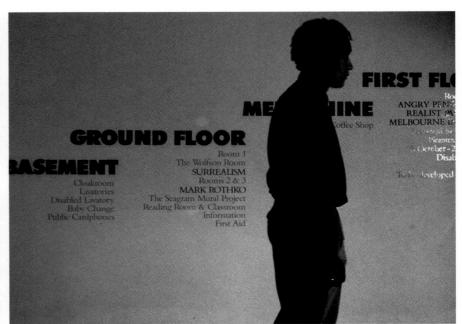

Designers
David Hillman, Jo Swindell
Design Firm
Pentagram Design Limited,
London, England
Client
Tate Gallery, Liverpool

In keeping with the building, which retains many of its original features, the signs were produced in cast iron and positioned flush to the walls. Secondary signs in black and grey used a classical typeface to complement the contents of the gallery. A series of mobile temporary signs were developed to indicate gallery closures, queuing points and directions to particular events. These free-standing signs comprised simple, brightly coloured symbols made of aluminium, mounted on tall steel rods attached to weighted steel bases.

Catalogue

Brochures

Exhibition poster

Exhibition poster

TATE GALLERY LIVERPOOL

*The National Collection of Modern Art
in the North of England*

Albert Dock, Liverpool L3 4BB

Winter Opening Hours, 1 October–31 March
Tuesday–Friday 11–5
Saturday, Sunday 11–6
Information Line 051-709 0507

The San Diego Hall of Champions is a sports museum located in Balboa Park, San Diego, California. Completed in 1982, it is dedicated to the celebration and commemoration of regional athletes who excelled at the national and international level of sports competitions. The ambience and image of the Hall is created out of sports materials as well as sports memorabilia. The Hall includes a theatre, a gift shop, a sports library, a conference room and administrative offices.

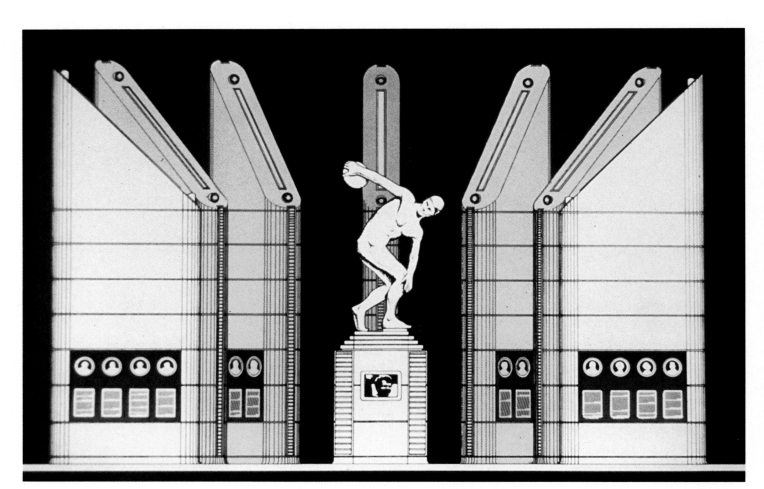

Designer
Joe C. Nicholson
Design Firm
Nicholson Design, Encinitas, California
Photographer
Sandra Williams
Client
San Diego Hall of Champions

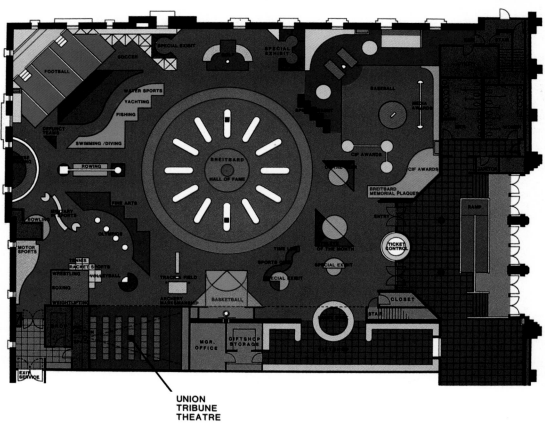

UNION
TRIBUNE
THEATRE

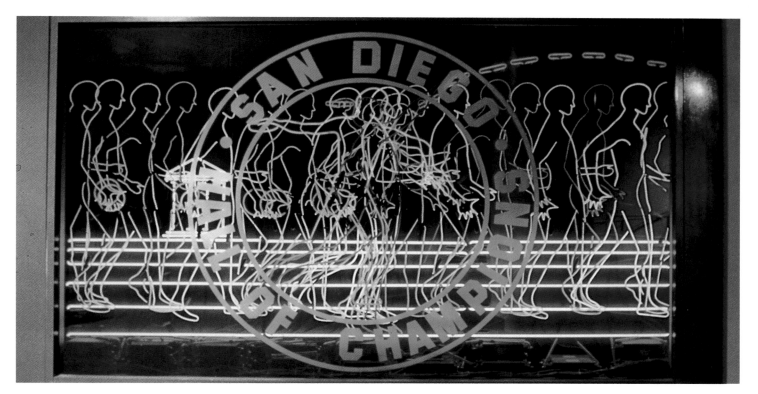

Whitechapel Art Gallery is London's leading contemporary art gallery.

The Gallery's logotype is a typographic expression of the gallery's rebuilding programme that preceded this new graphic identity. Brett Wickens' functional streamlining of classical letterforms symbolized the modernization of the gallery space itself.

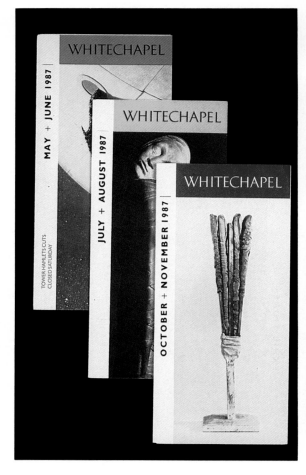

Event brochures

Designers
Peter Saville, Brett Wickens
Design Firm
Pentagram Design Limited,
London, England
Client
Whitechapel Art Gallery

Invitations

Exhibition poster

Exhibition catalogue

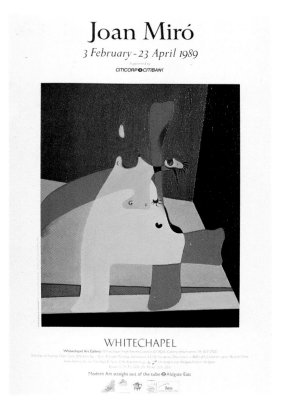

Designers
Peter Saville, Brett Wickens
Design Firm
Pentagram Design Limited,
London, England
Client
Whitechapel Art Gallery

American Museum of Natural History

The first phase of the new identity and signage system for the American Museum of Natural History was installed in 1992. It includes a new museum logo based on the architecture of the original building, five floor icons which combine floor numbers with graphic images, and a coordinated wayfinding system of signs and maps to help visitors find their way through the museum's 22 interconnected buildings which occupy six city blocks. Each exhibit floor has a "Loop", a circular base

path that leads through exhibit areas. Intersections lead to adjoining exhibit areas. The Loop is clearly shown on floor maps, and is marked throughout the museum by baseboard level "Loop Marker" signs. Floor maps are computer-generated for easy updating by the museum staff.

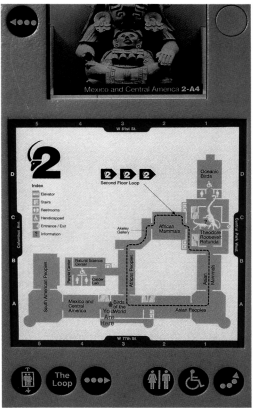

Art Director/Designer
Lance Wyman
Designers
Denise Guerra, Linda Iskander, Ralph Hertle
Design Firm
Lance Wyman Ltd., New York
Photographers
Denis Finnin, Craig Chesek, and AMNH
Sign Fabricator
M.T. Fuller

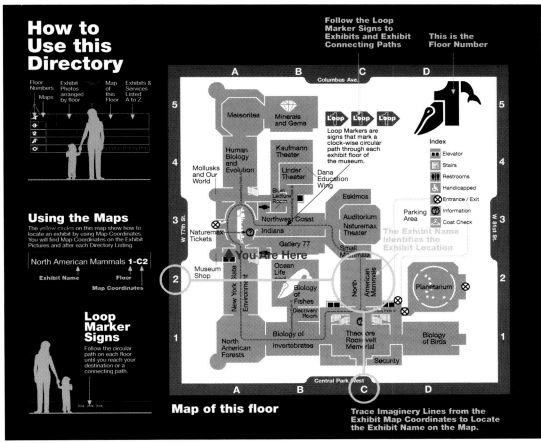

How to Use this Directory

Floor Numbers | Exhibit Photos arranged by floor | Map of this Floor | Exhibits & Services Listed A to Z

Maps

Using the Maps
The yellow circles on this map show how to locate an exhibit by using Map Coordinates. You will find Map Coordinates on the Exhibit Pictures and after each Directory Listing.

North American Mammals **1-C2**

Exhibit Name | Floor

Map Coordinates

Loop Marker Signs
Follow the circular path on each floor until you reach your destination or a connecting path.

Follow the Loop Marker Signs to Exhibits and Exhibit Connecting Paths

This is the Floor Number

Loop Loop Loop

Loop Markers are signs that mark a clock-wise circular path through each exhibit floor of the museum.

Index

Elevator
Stairs
Restrooms
Handicapped
Entrance / Exit
Information
Coat Check

The Exhibit Name Identifies the Exhibit Location

You Are Here

Map of this floor

Trace Imaginery Lines from the Exhibit Map Coordinates to Locate the Exhibit Name on the Map.

Built from the shell of an old power station, the Powerhouse is Australia's largest museum and the flagship of the Museum of Applied Arts and Sciences. Over 25 exhibitions take the visitor into human achievement, science and technology, the decorative arts, and the everyday lives of Australians. A visit can include fun with computer games, fascinating lectures, activities for children, classic films and provocative videos. Changing exhibits such as the Arnott's is an on-going program of the museum.

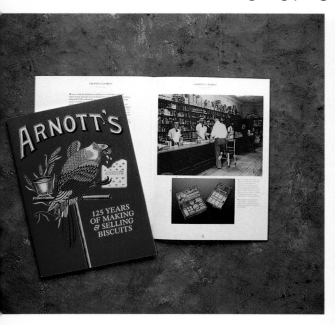

Art Director/Designer
John Spatchurst
Designers
Meryl Blundell, Romaine Joseph
Design Firm
Spatchurst Design Associates,
N.S.W., Australia
Copywriter
Powerhouse Museum
Client
Arnott's

Exhibition to commemorate Arnott's 125 years of making and selling biscuits

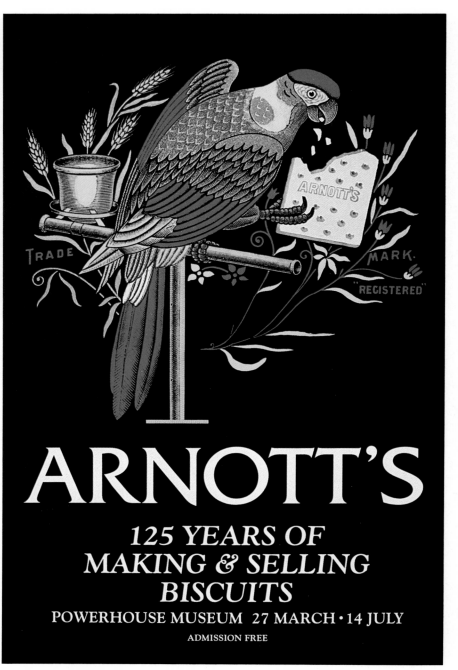

Since 1981, the Centre de design has been honouring its mandate to contribute to the development of a culture in design, on campus and beyond. Prestigious international exhibitions have made acclaimed stops within these walls.

The Centre also organizes conferences and seminars to encourage discussions over different aspects of design and has become an important actor in the ever changing world of international design.

Creative/Art Director
Frédéric Metz
Design Firm & Client
Centre de Design de l'Universite
du Québec, Canada
Illustrator/Photographer
Michel Brunelle

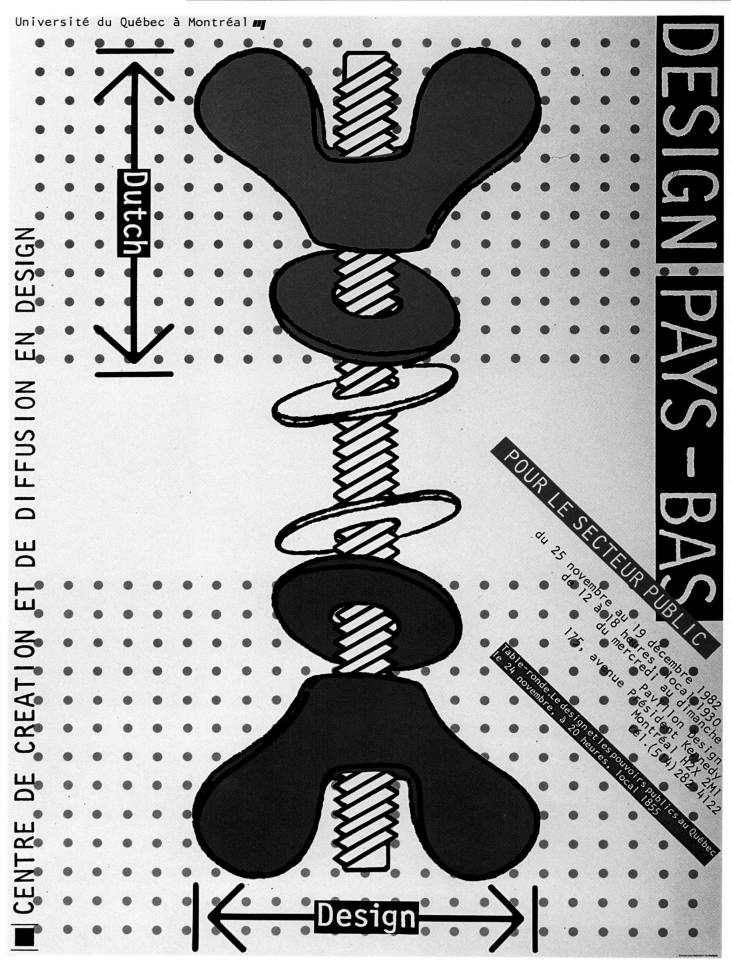

Designer
Alfred Halasa
Design Firm & Client
Centre de Design de l'Université
du Québec, Canada

EXHIBITIONNISME

(un document officiel, une pièce) devant l'autorité. ♦ 1° *Dr. proc*
V. Montrer, présenter, produire, représenter. *Exhiber ses fa*
papiers, ses titres, son passeport. ♦ 2° *Cour.* (XIVe). Montrer, ce
faire voir (à qqn, au public). *Montreur qui exhibe des singes,*
des ours. « Ainsi exhibé, il (un porte-monnaie) attire l'attentions
d'un vieux chemineau, qui me demande l'aumône » (LECOMTE).
♦ 3° Montrer avec ostentation ou impudeur. *Exhiber ses*
décorations, des toilettes tapageuses. V. Arborer, déployer
Finissants en design (déb. XXIe) *Exhiber sa science, ses vic*
V. Etalage, parade (faire). ◇ S'EXHIBER. *v. pron.* Se produ
se montrer en public. *« Il ne pouvait supporter de s'exh*
en public, d'être le point de mire de toute une société » (R.
◇ ANT. *Cacher, dissimuler.*
EXHIBITION [ɛgzibisjɔ̃]. *n. f.* (XIIe ; lat. *exhibitio*).
d'exhiber. ♦ 1° *Dr.* Présentation (d'une pièce). *Ex*
Vernissage — *Par ext.* Exposition, représentati
Mercredi soir 24 avril (*spécialt.* au public). Impudeur.
de 17 à 19 heures. ♦ Fait d'afficher *« Comme un h*
V. Déploiement, étalage, montre, parade. Arborer
4 jours de midi à 18 heures V. Présentation, *qui va f*
25, 26, 27, 28 avril 1985. *Exhibition de toiles, de m*
Centre de création et de diffusion en design exhibitionnism
200 ouest, rue Sherbrooke, Montréal Produire avec os
tél. 514/282 3395 Montrer, *comme dans un cirque.*
■ Université du Québec à Montréal

[ɛgzibisjɔnism(ə)]. *n. m*
exhibition). ♦ 1° *Méd.* Obsession morbide qui
tains sujets à exhiber leurs organes génitaux. –
Goût de se montrer tout nu. ♦ 2° *Fig.* Fait d
public ses sentiments, sa vie privée, ce qu'on
Exhibitionnisme d'un écrivain.
EXHIBITIONNISTE [ɛgzibisjɔn
Personne atteinte d'exhibitionni
Personne qui aime se montre
exhibitionniste.
EXHIBER [ɛgzibe]
Produire (un docum
V. Montrer, présent

Art Director
Frédéric Metz
Designer
Serge Cassan
Design Firm & Client
Centre de Design de l'Université
du Québec, Canada

Designer
Alfred Halasa
Design Firm & Client
Centre de Design de l'Université
du Québec, Canada

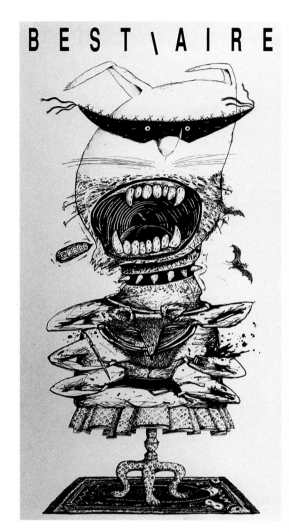

Art Director/Designer
Gérard Bochud
Design Firm & Client
Université du Québec à
Montreal, Canada
Illustrators/Photographers
Marie Louise Gay, Normand
Cousineau, Phillippe Beha,
Michelle Lemieux
Copywriter
BCR Litho

Creative/Art Director
Frédéric Metz
Designer
Pier Savard
Design Firm & Client
Centre de Design de l'Université
du Québec, Canada

Creative/Art Director
Gérard Bochud
Designers
Tintin, Escher, Copernic
Design Firm & Client
Université du Québec à
Montreal, Canada
Copywriter
BCR Litho

Creative/Art Director
Frédéric Metz
Designer
Lynn Lefebvre
Design Firm & Client
Centre de Design de l'Université
du Québec, Canada
Illustrator
Alain Pilon
Copywriter
Frédéric Metz

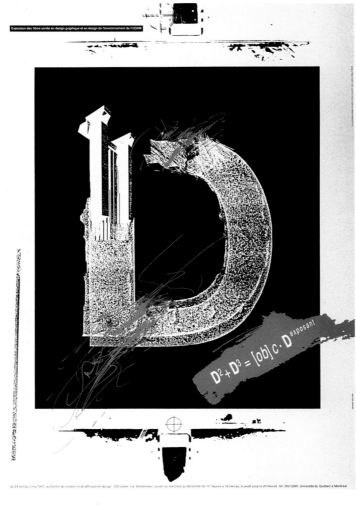

Designer
Alfred Halasa
Design Firm & Client
Centre de Design de l'Université
du Québec, Canada

Art Director
Gérard Bochud
Designers
O. Fantini, H. Lussier, S. Cloutier
Design Firm & Client
Université du Québec à
Montreal, Canada
Copywriter
BCR Litho

"Friendship One" – a Boeing 747 SP – set out to break the around-the-world record flight for a civilian aircraft and raise funds for a group of children's organization. The modular exhibit, "Mission Control", was located at the Museum of Flight in Seattle, and was used as a base to monitor the progress of the airplane's flight. Applications included: exhibit design and banners; letterhead; press kits; t-shirts, sweatshirts and lab coats; membership pins.

Art Director
Jack Anderson
Designers
Jack Anderson, Mike Courtney, Mary Hermes, Jani Drewfs, Julie Tanagi-Lock
Design Firm
Hornall Anderson Design Works, Seattle, Washington
Illustrator
Jack Anderson
Client
Museum of Flight

The Art Gallery of New South Wales was established in 1871. Today it presents outstanding permanent collections of Australian, Aboriginal, Asian, European and Contemporary art together with a lively programme of national and international temporary exhibitions. The Gallery presents a wealth of public programmes including lectures, workshops and events and offers a wide range of visitor services including theatres, cafes and the Gallery Shop. The Gallery continues to produce substantial exhibition catalogues and books.

Art Director/Designer
John Spatchurst
Design Firm
Spatchurst Design Associates,
N.S.W., Australia
Client
Art Gallery of New South Wales

Art Director/Designer
Steven Joseph
Design Firm
Spatchurst Design Associates,
N.S.W., Australia
Client
Art Gallery of New South Wales

Art Director/Designer
John Spatchurst
Design Firm
Spatchurst Design Associates,
N.S.W., Australia
Client
Art Gallery of New South Wales

Art Director
John Spatchurst
Designer
Meryl Blundell
Design Firm
Spatchurst Design Associates,
N.S.W., Australia
Client
Art Gallery of New South Wales

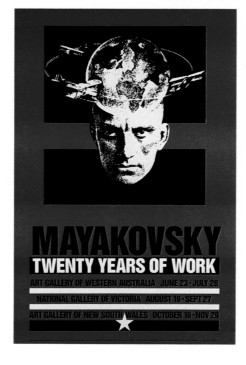

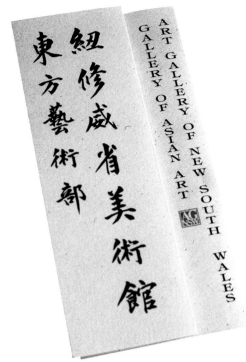

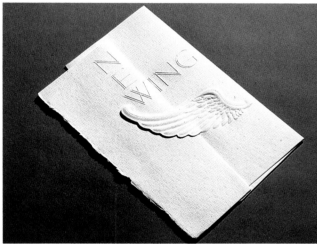

Art Director/Designer
John Spatchurst
Design Firm
Spatchurst Design Associates,
N.S.W., Australia
Photographer
F. Adriani
Client
Art Gallery of New South Wales

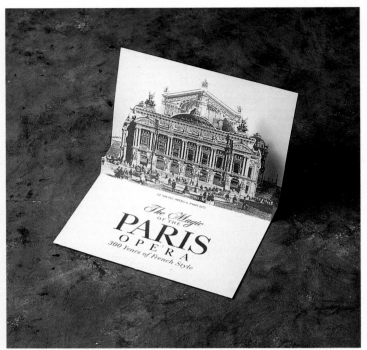

Art Director/Designer
John Spatchurst
Design Firm
Spatchurst Design Associates,
N.S.W., Australia
Client
Art Gallery of New South Wales

Art Director
John Spatchurst
Designer
Meryl Blundell
Design Firm
Spatchurst Design Associates,
N.S.W., Australia
Client
Art Gallery of New South Wales

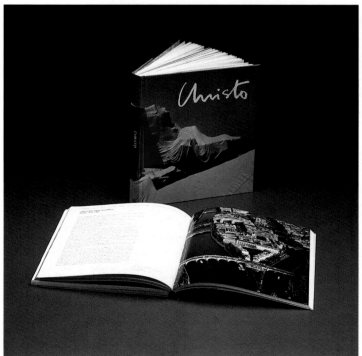

Art Director
John Spatchurst
Designer
Sarah Drury
Design Firm
Spatchurst Design Associates,
N.S.W., Australia
Client
Art Gallery of New South Wales

Art Director
John Spatchurst
Designer
Meryl Blundell
Design Firm
Spatchurst Design Associates,
N.S.W., Australia
Photographer
Keiichi Tahara
Client
Art Gallery of New South Wales

Art Director/Designer
John Spatchurst
Designer
Meryl Blundell
Design Firm
Spatchurst Design Associates,
N.S.W., Australia
Copywriter
Public Programmes, Art Gallery
of N.S.W.
Client
Art Gallery of New South Wales

A wayfinding system of symbols, signs and maps installed to help visitors find their way to the monuments, memorials and museums on and around the Washington Mall. The program includes symbol/banners, a series of kiosks, three dimensional maps keyed in five languages, and handout maps for the Smithsonian Institution and National Park Service. Porcelain enamelled symbol/banners suspended from Olmstead lamp poles create a visual index, identifying the points of interest as they run down either side of the Mall.

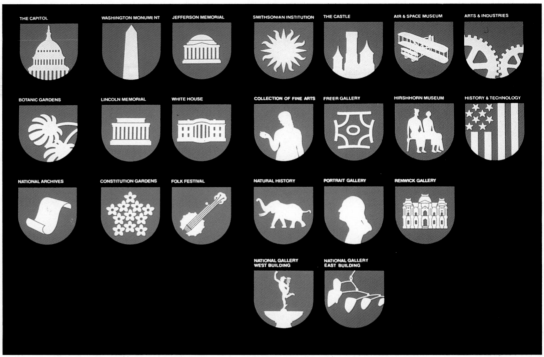

Art Directors/Designers
Lance Wyman, Bill Cannan
Designers
Brian Flahive, Tucker Viemeister, Tom DeMonse, Francisco Gallardo
Design Firm
Wyman & Cannan Co.,
New York
Architects
Skidmore, Owings & Merrill, Washington
Fabricators
Jack Stone, Smithsonian Institution, Ervite Corp., Charles Boye, Cherokee Construction Co.

IOWA ARTS Council

DIRECTION

Discover a NEW

WAKE UP to the ARTS!

TOURING Arts TEAM

Art Director/Designer
John Sayles
Design Firm
Sayles Graphic Design,
Des Moines, Iowa
Illustrator
John Sayles
Copywriter
Wendy Lyons
Client
Iowa Arts Council

*The Touring Arts Team is a
troupe of visual artists who visit
small Iowa communities.*

Designer
Kijuro Yahagi
Design Firm
Kijuro Yahagi, Tokyo, Japan
Illustrator
Kijuro Yahagi
Client
Kawasaki City Museum

Designer
Kijuro Yahagi
Design Firm
Kijuro Yahagi, Tokyo, Japan
Illustrator
Kijuro Yahagi
Client
Kawasaki City Museum

Designer
Kijuro Yahagi
Design Firm
Kijuro Yahagi, Tokyo, Japan
Illustrator
Kijuro Yahagi
Client
Kawasaki City Museum

La Biennale di Venezia/XLIV Esposizione Internazionale d'Arte 1990
The XLIVth International Art Exhibition of the Venice Biennale 1990

Padiglione Giapponese, Giardini di Castello   Presentato dalla Japan Foundation   Japanese Pavilion, Giardini di Castello   Presented by the Japan Foundation

ENDO Toshikatsu

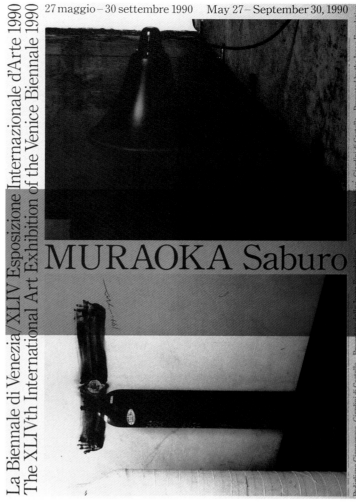

La Biennale di Venezia/XLIV Esposizione Internazionale d'Arte 1990
The XLIVth International Art Exhibition of the Venice Biennale 1990

Padiglione Giapponese, Giardini di Castello   Presentato dalla Japan Foundation   Japanese Pavilion, Giardini di Castello   Presented by the Japan Foundation

MURAOKA Saburo

Designer
Kijuro Yahagi
Design Firm
Kijuro Yahagi, Tokyo, Japan
Client
The Japan Foundation

Designer
Kijuro Yahagi
Design Firm
Kijuro Yahagi, Tokyo, Japan
Client
The Japan Foundation

Designer
Kijuro Yahagi
Design Firm
Kijuro Yahagi, Tokyo, Japan
Client
Meguro Museum of Art, Tokyo

'85 HINUMA

「'85涸沼・土の光景」

開催日程：
1985年9月21日［土］—10月6日［日］
開催会場：
茨城県東茨城郡茨城町大字中石崎宇宮前2303
涸沼宮前荘敷地

主催：「'85涸沼・土の光景」実行委員会
後援：茨城県、茨城県教育委員会、水戸市、笠間市、常澄村、茨城町、内原町、大洗町、
友部町、岩間町、七会村、旭村（涸沼関連市町村）
茨城新聞社、茨城放送局、NHK水戸放送局
協賛：茨城県商工会連合会、茨城県商工会議所連合会、
茨城県建築士会、茨城県建築設計監理協会、茨城県建築士事務所協会、笠間日動美術館
技術協力：茨城県工業センター窯業指導所
●展示部門：
[1]土への取組—現代美術の作家が「土」への新たな取組を試みる部門
[企画顧問]中原佑介［企画委員］たにあらた、中村英樹、矢口國夫
[参加作家]井田照一、榎倉康二、遠藤利克、河口龍夫、川島清、
北辻良央、城戸孝充、熊谷優子、久里洋二、黒川弘毅、篠田守男、宿沢育夫、
菅野由美子、杉山知子、関口敦仁、高見澤文夫、辰野登恵子、
中西夏之、中原浩大、摩坂尚嘉、堀浩哉、眞板雅文、松井智惠、
向井美恵、最上壽之、矢野美智子、横尾忠則、李禹煥、
渡辺豊重（以上60資順）沈文燮（特別参加）
[2]土からの取組—土を素材として活躍するクレイ・ワークの作家の部門
[企画顧問]乾由明［企画委員］辻晋代治、福永重樹
[参加作家]槇松永太、小倉亨、笹山忠保、佐藤敏、沢田佳予子、重松あゆみ、
杉浦康益、高野基夫、田嶋悦子、堤展子、中村錦平、星野暁、松井紫朗、
松田百合子、森野泰明、横原睦夫、山田修作、吉川正道、吉竹弘
[3]土・地域から—地元作家（主として常磐線沿線に根を張る作家）の部門
[参加作家]浅田恵美子、石井敏子、伊藤公象、伊庭知香、串山久美子、小林三千夫、小林優子、
土門邦映、緑川宏樹、横尾聡
[4]建築と土の造形—建築と土の関わりを示す部門
[参加建築案]若山滋・地元建築家グループ
●イベント：シンポジウム、パフォーマンス
9月22日［日］、23日［月・祝］、27日［金］、28日［土］、29日［日］

「'85涸沼・土の光景」実行委員会
事務局：笠間市本戸6097-1伊藤公象方tel.02967-4-4035
実行委員：伊藤公象、伊藤知香、内田芳季、海老沢康郎、小林三千夫、小林優子、戸頃志帆、市篤宏、墻谷昭則
制作協力：神谷武、諸城洋子、高瀬豊、長田静香、松原明美、松村喜代子、木木久美子

Designer
Kijuro Yahagi
Design Firm
Kijuro Yahagi, Tokyo, Japan

Client
1985 Hinuma Committee

Close-up of Japan

NEW YORK 1985–6

NEW YORK SYMPHONIC ENSEMBLE CONCERT
conducted by MAMORU TAKAHARA
Nov. 17, 1985 at Alice Tully Hall, Lincoln Center

KAZUO OHNO & KUNIKO KISANUKI
Contemporary Dance in Japan
Nov. 19–24, 1985 at the Joyce Theater

NEW FILMS/ANIMATION
Jan. 9–Feb. 7, 1986 at The Japan Film Center
and The Museum of Modern Art

NEW VIDEO : JAPAN
Jan. 16–Feb. 28, 1986 at The Museum of Modern Art

THE MITSUI GROUP

Designer
Kijuro Yahagi
Design Firm
Kijuro Yahagi, Tokyo, Japan

Client
The Mitsui Group

Designer
Kijuro Yahagi
Design Firm
Kijuro Yahagi, Tokyo, Japan
Client
Tokyo Tower Project Committee

Designer
Kijuro Yahagi
Design Firm
Kijuro Yahagi, Tokyo, Japan
Client
The Japan Foundation

Designer
Kijuro Yahagi
Design Firm
Kijuro Yahagi, Tokyo, Japan
Client
The Japan Foundation

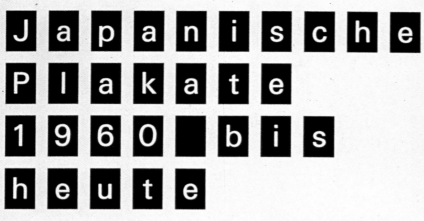

Japanische Plakate 1960 bis heute

26. Oktober 1988
bis 15. Januar 1989
Dienstag bis Sonntag
10 bis 17 Uhr
Die Neue Sammlung
Prinzregentenstrasse 3
München

Designer
Pierre Mendell
Design Firm
Mendell & Oberer, Munich,
Germany

Client
Die Neue Sammlung (Museum
for Applied Art, Munich)

An exhibit of Japanese Posters

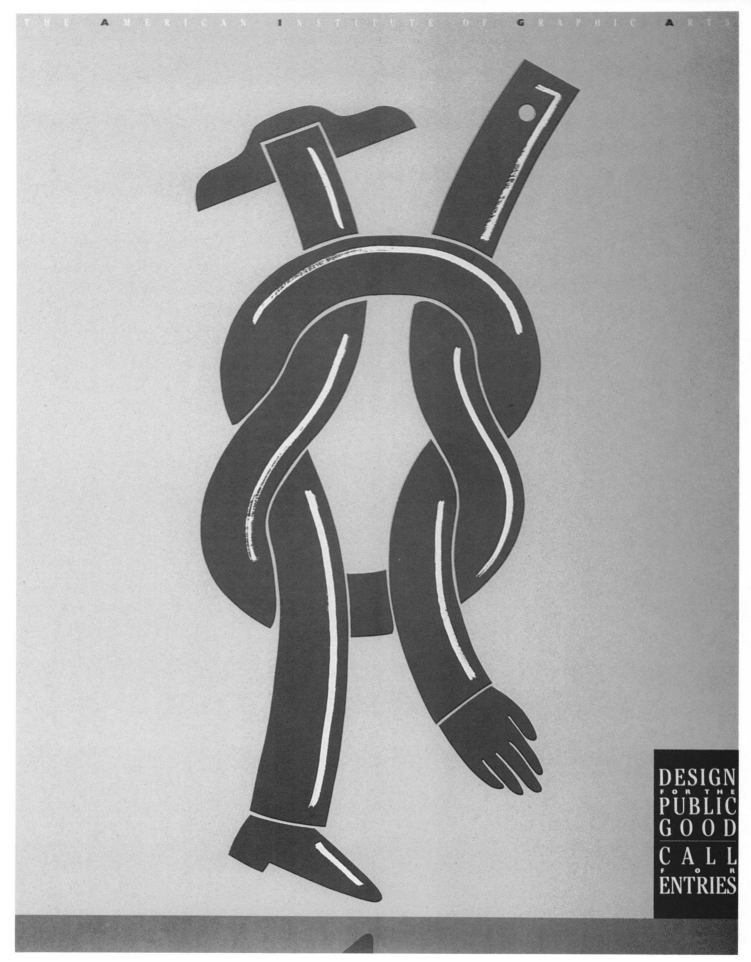

DESIGN
FOR THE
PUBLIC
GOOD
CALL
FOR
ENTRIES

Art Director
Lanny Sommese
Designer
Kristin Breslin
Design Firm
Sommese Design, State College,
Pennsylvania

Illustrator
Lanny Sommese
Copywriter
Lanny Sommese
Client
American Institute of Graphics
Arts, New York

Die Neue Sammlung
München

Staatliches Museum für
angewandte Kunst
Design des
19. und 20. Jahrhunderts

"I love design"
Entwurf: Mendell & Oberer

Design
Process
Auto

22.11.86 –
8.2.87

Designer
Pierre Mendell
Design Firm
Mendell & Oberer, Munich,
Germany
Client
Die Neue Sammlung (Museum
for Applied Art, Munich)

(Translation) I Love Design

Designer
Pierre Mendell
Design Firm
Mendell & Oberer, Munich,
Germany
Client
Die Neue Sammlung (Museum
for Applied Art, Munich)

*An exhibit on the design process
in automobiles*

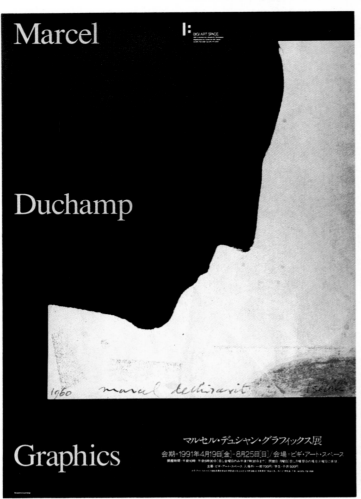

Designer
Kijuro Yahagi
Design Firm
Kijuro Yahagi, Tokyo, Japan
Client
BIGI Art Space

Designer
Kijuro Yahagi
Design Firm
Kijuro Yahagi, Tokyo, Japan
Client
BIGI Art Space

Designer
Michaël Snitker
Design Firm
Proforma Rotterdam,
The Netherlands
Client
Teylers Museum, Haarlem

lost/FOUND

lost/FOUND is a series of exhibitions that investigate the usage and application of cultural, consumer and/or social castoffs through the context of language, objects and sound.

Curator: Michael Willse
Exhibitions Coordinator: Amy Orr

Lawrence Gallery
Rosemont College
Montgomery Avenue
Rosemont, PA 19010
(215) 527-0200

Gallery Hours:
Monday–Friday 9–5 pm
Saturday 9–1 pm

lost/FOUND LANGUAGE:
The use of language as visual or conceptual component, deriving directly or indirectly from popular culture.

November 5—December 2
Opening Reception:
Friday, November 7, 8–10 pm

lost/FOUND OBJECTS:
The object used directly or in its appropriated state. The object presented with intervention by the artist.

January 7—February 4
Opening Reception:
Friday, January 9, 8–10 pm

lost/FOUND SOUND:
The investigation of sound as subject. Sound as an incorporated aspect of the art object. A cross disciplinary approach/exploration of sound/music.

March 4—March 31
Opening Reception:
Friday, March 6, 8–10 pm

Supported, in part, by the
Pennsylvania Council on the Arts

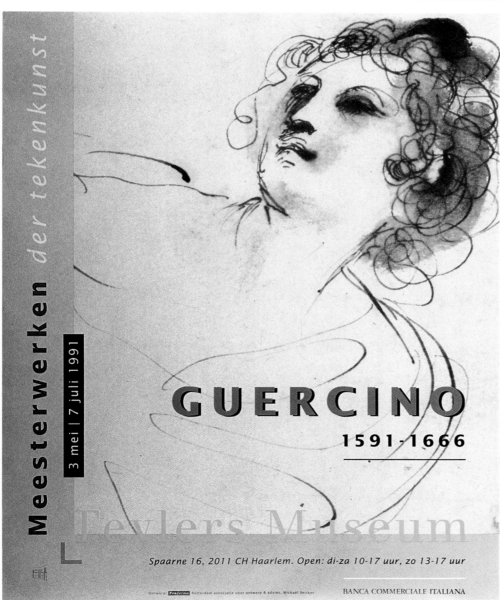

Designers
Joe Scorsone, Alice Drueding
Design Firm
Scorsone/Drueding, Jenkintown, Pennsylvania
Illustrator/Photographer
Joe Scorsone, Alice Drueding
Copywriter
Amy Orr
Client
Rosemont College (Lawrence Gallery)

Lost/Found was a series of exhibitions that investigated the usage and application of cultural, consumer and/or social castoffs through the context of language, objects and sound.

Designer
Michaël Snitker
Design Firm
Proforma Rotterdam,
The Netherlands
Client
Teylers Museum, Haarlem

Art Director
John Brady
Designer
Rick Madison
Design Firm
John Brady Design Consultants,
Pittsburgh, Pennsylvania
Photographer
Tom Gigliotti
Client
Westmoreland Museum of Art

Art Director/Designer
Edi Berk
Design Firm
KROG, Ljubljana, Slovenija
Photographer
Dragan Arrigler
Client
Gallery INSULA, Ljubljana

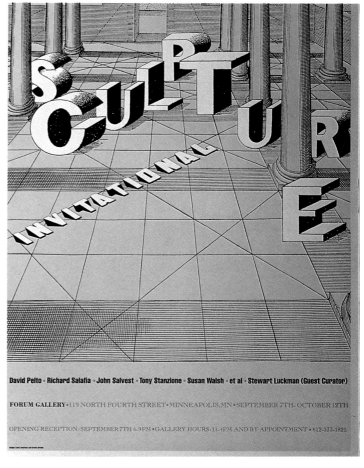

Designer/Illustrator
Lanny Sommese
Design Firm
Sommese Design, State College,
Pennsylvania
Client
Forum Gallery, Minneapolis

Designer/Illustrator
Lanny Sommese
Design Firm
Sommese Design, State College,
Pennsylvania
Client
Bill Mayer - Artist

Designer/Illustrator
Lanny Sommese
Design Firm
Sommese Design, State College,
Pennsylvania
Client
Depree Art Center, Hope College

Designer/Illustrator
Lanny Sommese
Designer
Kristin Breslin
Design Firm
Sommese Design, State College,
Pennsylvania
Client
Forum Gallery, Minneapolis

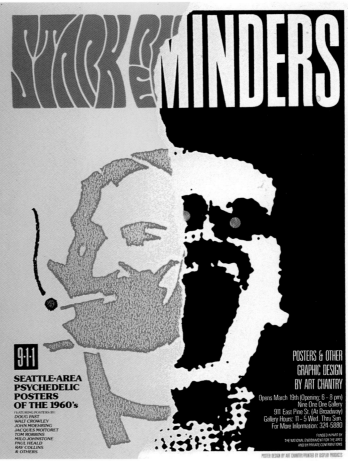

Designer
Art Chantry
Design Firm
Art Chantry, Seattle, Washington
Photographer
Tom Collicott
Client
School of Visual Concepts

Designer
Art Chantry
Design Firm
Art Chantry, Seattle, Washington
Illustrator
Art Chantry
Client
911

Designer
Lanny Sommese
Design Firm
Sommese Design, State College, Pennsylvania
Client
Macalester Gallery

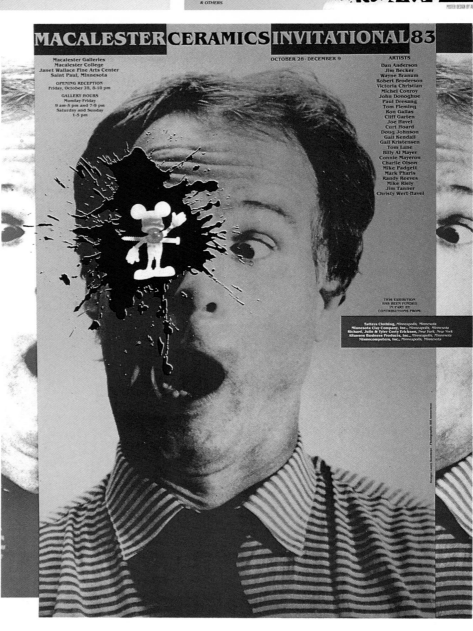

Designer
Art Chantry
Design Firm
Art Chantry, Seattle, Washington

Illustrator
Carl Smool
Client
Rod Stuart Inc.

Poster glows in the dark

Designer/Illustrator
Lanny Sommese
Design Firm
Sommese Design, State College, Pennsylvania
Client
Forum Gallery, Minneapolis

Designer/Illustrator
Art Chantry
Design Firm
Art Chantry, Seattle, Washington
Copywriter
Susan Purves
Client
Center on Contemporary Art

Designer
Art Chantry
Design Firm
Art Chantry, Seattle, Washington
Illustrator
T. Michael Gardiner
Client
One Reel/Bumbershoot

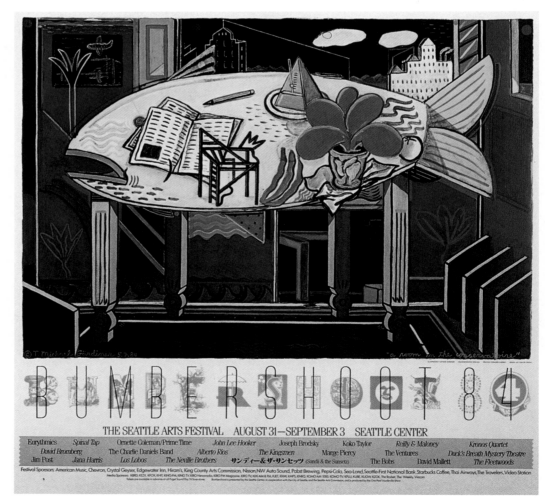

DESIGN
IST KUNST
DIE SICH
NÜTZLICH
MACHT

Quilts der
Amischen
17.4.–2.6.91
Die Neue
Sammlung

THE

REAL

ART

OF

FAKE

FOOD

Design by Takaaki Matsumoto

MAY 24-

JULY 16

AT

GALLERY

91

Gallery 91
91 Grand Street
New York, NY 10013

Designer
Pierre Mendell
Design Firm
Mendell & Oberer, Munich,
Germany
Copywriter
Carlos Obers
Client
Die Neue Sammlung (Museum
for Applied Art, Munich)

*(Translation) Design is art that
makes itself useful*

Designer
Pierre Mendell
Design Firm
Mendell & Oberer, Munich,
Germany
Client
Die Neue Sammlung (Museum
for Applied Art, Munich)

An exhibit of Amish Quiltsat

Designer
Takaaki Matsumoto
Design Firm
M Plus M Incorporated,
New York
Client
Gallery 91

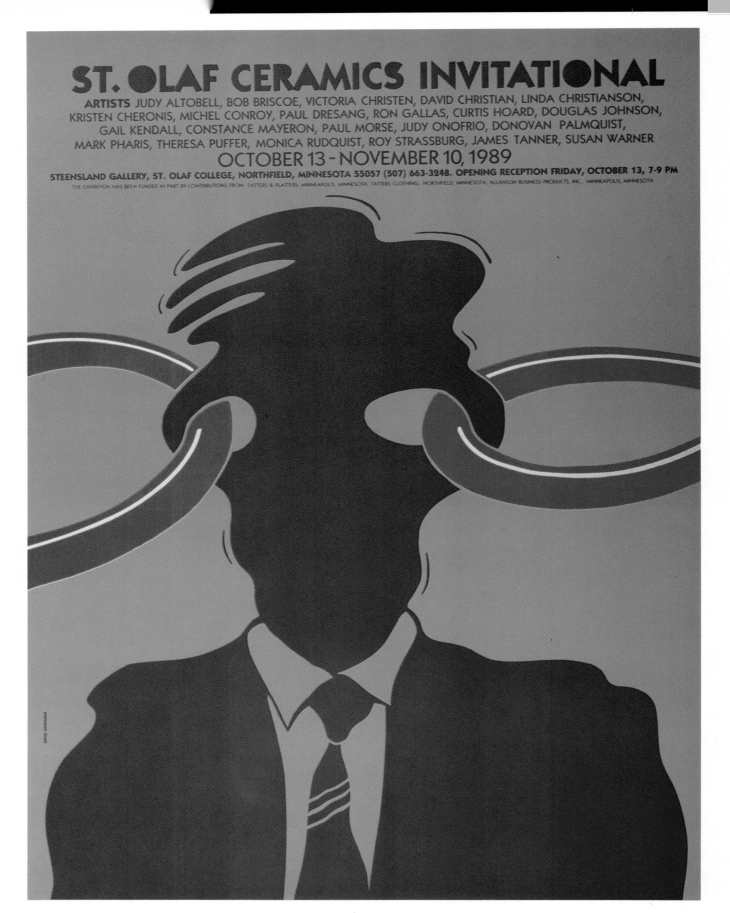

Designer/Illustrator
Lanny Sommese
Design Firm
Sommese Design, State College,
Pennsylvania
Client
Steensland Gallery, St. Olaf
College, Minneapolis

Art Director/Illustrator
Gregory Oznowich
Designers
Gregory Oznowich, S. Jeffrey
Prugh, Mary Jane Parente/Smith
Design Firm
Watt, Roop & Co., Cleveland,
Ohio
Client
The Cleveland Chapter of the
American Institute of Graphic Arts

*In October of 1989, the Soviet
government offered an
unprecedented opportunity to
U.S. citizens -- a chance to view
contemporary Soviet life through
the loan of over 75 posters, all
created within the last three
years. The Cleveland Chapter of
the American Institute of Graphic
Arts was one of 12 chapters
within the U.S.A. to host this
show of poster art never before
seen outside the Soviet Union.*

POSTER ART OF THE SOVIET UNION: A WINDOW INTO SOVIET LIFE

Presented by the Cleveland Chapter of the American Institute of Graphic Arts.

Monday July 29 through Friday August 23, at the Cleveland State University Art Gallery, 2307 Chester Avenue. Gallery hours: Monday through Friday 9:00 am to 5:00 pm.

This tour was made possible by AIGA, San Diego after a year's worth of coordination and effort with the Union of Soviet Artists. This travelling exhibition is an achievement of AIGA, San Diego Chapter (619.232.2888), ARETE Magazine, Gallery Services/Artrageous and Mon Van Moving Services/Allied Van Lines (800.222.8290).

AIGA

Design: Gregory Oznowich, Watt, Roop & Co.   Printing: Fortran Printing   Imaging: Typemasters, Inc.   Photostats: Technograph Media Services Inc.   Paper: Alling and Cory

Designer/Illustrator
Lanny Sommese
Design Firm
Sommese Design, State College,
Pennsylvania
Client
Depree Art Center & Gallery

Designer
Lanny Sommese
Design Firm
Sommese Design, State College,
Pennsylvania
Client
Herman Miller

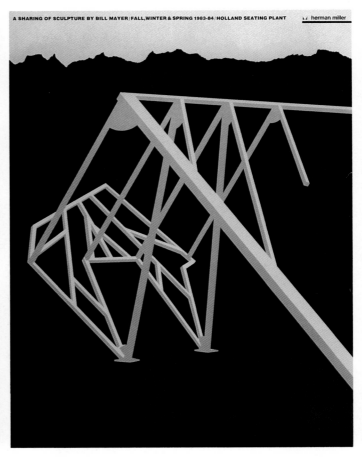

Designer
Michaël Snitker
Design Firm
Proforma Rotterdam,
The Netherlands
Client
Kunstlijn

*Big art exhibition in galleries in
Haarlem*

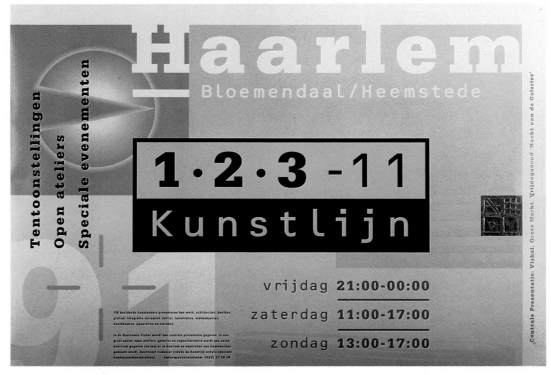

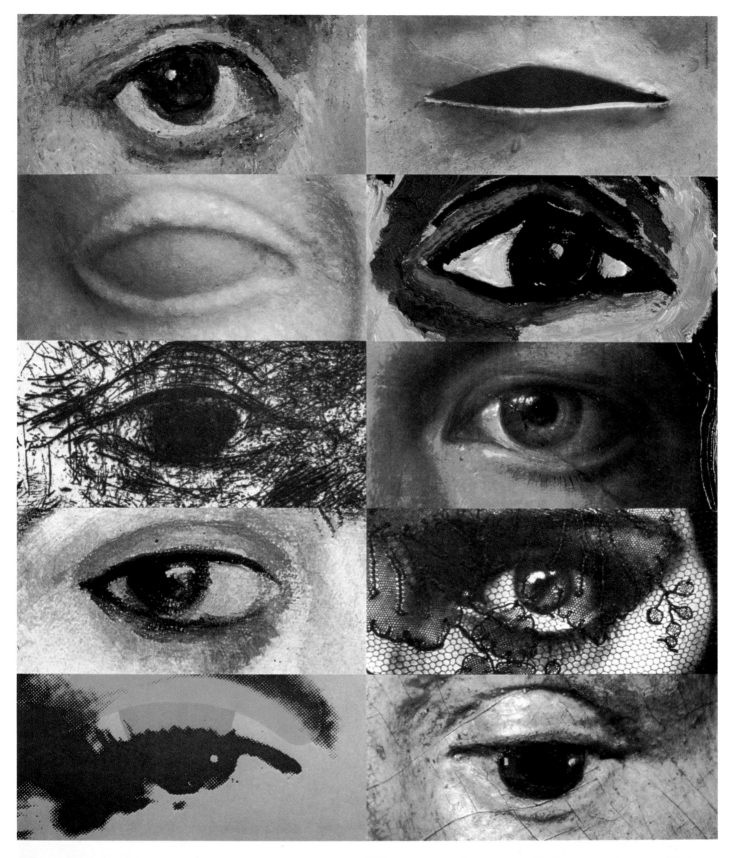

Kunst öffnet die Augen.

Besuchen Sie Bayerns Staatliche Museen.

Designer
Pierre Mendell
Design Firm
Mendell & Oberer, Munich, Germany

Client
Bayerische Staatsgemälde Sammlungen

Poster for 10 art museums in Munich
(Translation) Art opens the eyes

Design Firm
Chermayeff & Geismar Inc.,
New York
Client
Mobil

Mobil Corporation has for over 20 years supported extraordinary art and cultural exhibitions and theatrical television productions. Not only do they support these events, but publicize them with posters and advertising which are equally uncommercial. It is corporate support of the arts at its best.

Visit the Cooper-Hewitt Museum of Design. MTA gets you there.

Subway: ④⑤⑥ to 86 St. (Museum: 91st & 5th)
Bus: M1 M2 M3 M4 Culture Bus Loop 1 (Stop 13)
Transit Information: (212) 330-1234

Ⓜ Metropolitan Transportation Authority

Provided as a public service by Mobil

Visit The Brooklyn Museum. MTA gets you there.

Subway: ②③ (Eastern Pwy-Bklyn Mus) ⑤⑤ (Botanic Gdns-Eastern Pwy)
Bus: B41 B45 B48 B69 Culture Bus Loop 2 (Stop 9)
Transit Information: (212) 330-1234

Ⓜ Metropolitan Transportation Authority

Provided as a public service by Mobil

Visit the Museum of the City of New York. MTA gets you there.

Subway: ⑥ (103rd Street)
Bus: M1 M2 M3 M4 Culture Bus Loop 1 (Stop 12)
Transit Information: (212) 330-1234

Ⓜ Metropolitan Transportation Authority

Provided as a public service by Mobil

The Temple
of Dendur
in the new
Sackler Wing
will be open
to the public
Thursday evenings
Sept 28-Nov 16
The Metropolitan
Museum of Art
Fifth Ave & 82nd St
Made possible
by a grant
from Mobil

Greek Art of the Aegean Islands

**Nov 1 through Feb 10, 1980
The Metropolitan Museum of Art
Fifth Avenue at 82nd Street**

Supported by a grant from Mobil

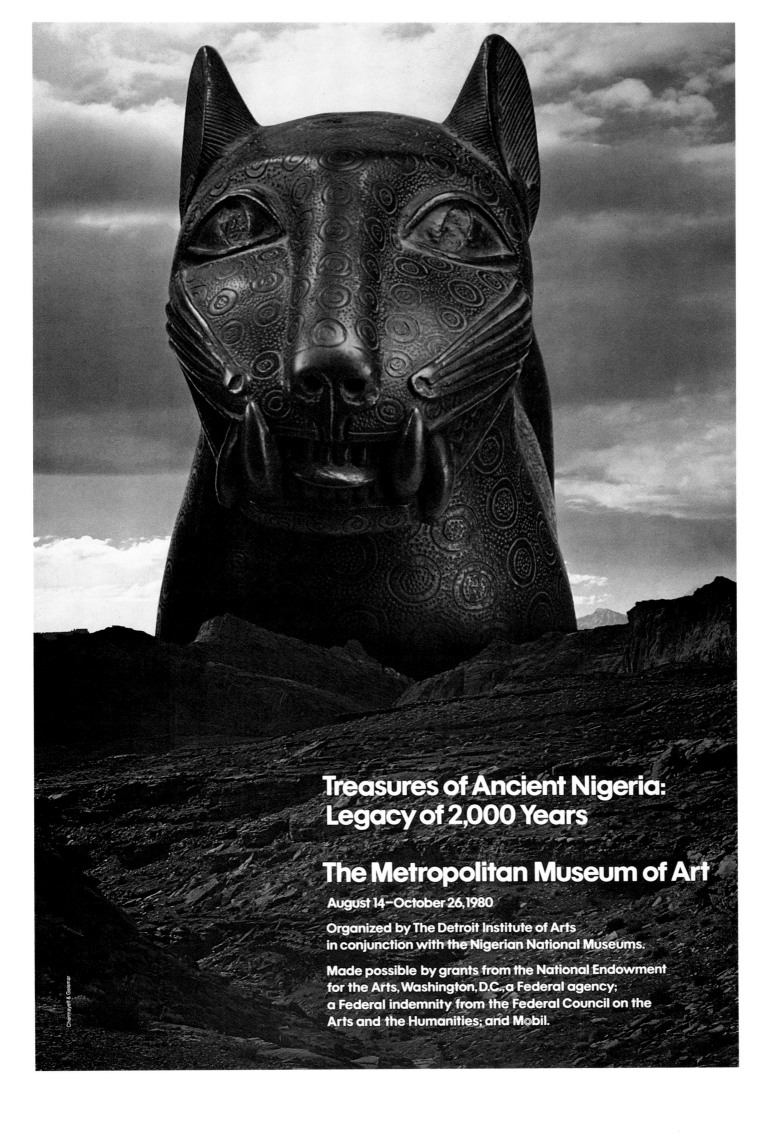

Treasures of Ancient Nigeria: Legacy of 2,000 Years

The Metropolitan Museum of Art

August 14–October 26, 1980

Organized by The Detroit Institute of Arts
in conjunction with the Nigerian National Museums.

Made possible by grants from the National Endowment
for the Arts, Washington, D.C., a Federal agency;
a Federal indemnity from the Federal Council on the
Arts and the Humanities; and Mobil.

Chermayeff & Geismar

Treasures of Ancient Nigeria: Legacy of 2,000 Years

The Detroit Institute of Arts

January 17–March 16, 1980

**Organized by The Detroit Institute of Arts
in conjunction with the Nigerian National Museums.**

**Made possible by grants from the National Endowment
for the Arts, Washington, D.C., a Federal agency;
a Federal indemnity from the Federal Council on the
Arts and the Humanities; and Mobil.**

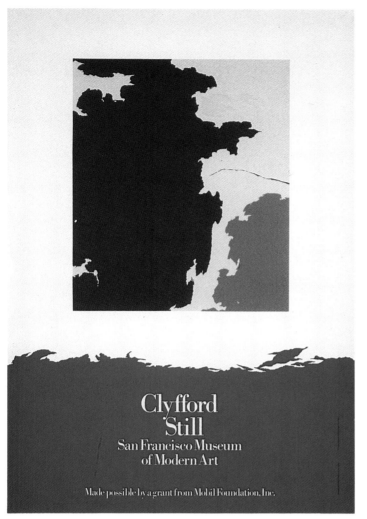

Clyfford
Still
San Francisco Museum
of Modern Art

Made possible by a grant from Mobil Foundation, Inc.

IMAGES OF AN ERA THE AMERICAN POSTER 1945-75

Grey Art Gallery & Study Center   New York University

May 22-June 30
100 Washington Square

Organized by the National Collection of Fine Arts,
Smithsonian Institution
Made possible by a grant from Mobil

Whitney Museum of American Art   75th & Madison   open free Tuesday evenings

Made
possible
by a grant from
Mobil Oil
Corporation

GUGGENHEIM
MUSEUM
OPEN FREE TUESDAY
EVENINGS

89th St & 5th Ave
5 to 8 pm
Made possible
by a grant from Mobil

An Exhibition of Ceremonial Robes
of the Imperial Court
from the Palace Museum, Peking,
People's Republic of China
September 24 thru October 21
Bloomingdale's   1000 Third Avenue,
Made possible by a grant from Mobil

Chermayeff & Geismar

Maori Art from New Zealand Collections — An exhibition organized by The American Federation of Arts — The Metropolitan Museum of Art September 11–January 6, 1985 — Made possible by a grant from Mobil

TE MAORI

Organized in association with the New Zealand Government, the Maori people, and the New Zealand lending museums. Supported by the National Endowment for the Arts, the National Endowment for the Humanities, an indemnity from the Federal Council on the Arts and Humanities, Air New Zealand, and National Patrons of The American Federation of Arts.

Gateway of Pukeroa Fort (detail) Auckland Institute and Museum, Auckland, New Zealand   Photo: ©1983 New Zealand Government   Design: Chermayeff & Geismar Associates

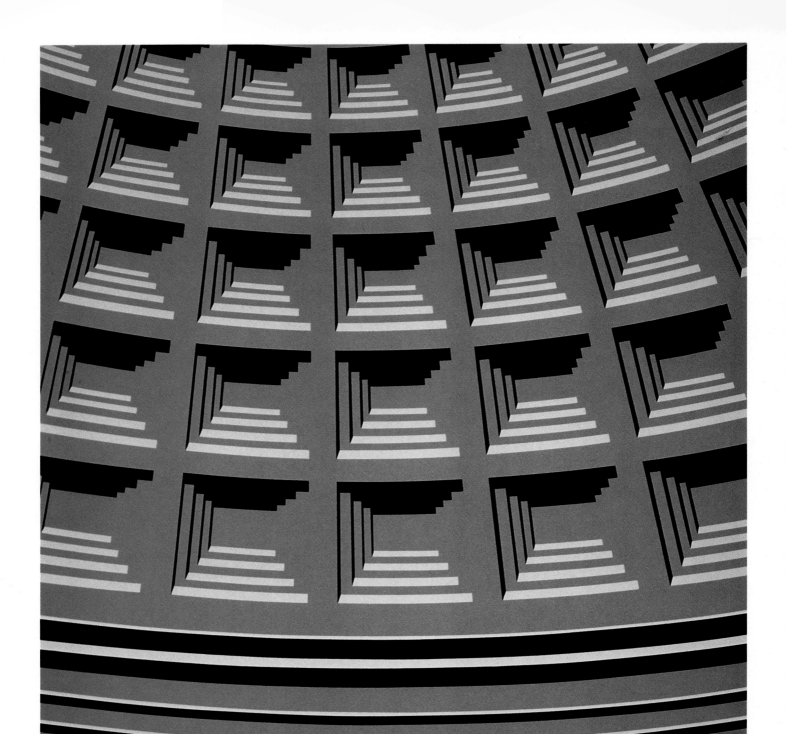

CORCORAN GALLERY OF ART
17TH ST. & NEW YORK AVE. N.W.
OPEN FREE THURSDAYS 4:30-9PM
MADE POSSIBLE BY A GRANT FROM MOBIL

Chermayeff & Geismar

Evenings at four museums

Summergarden at MOMA — Friday, Saturday, & Sunday evenings June 2–Sept 3

Whitney — Each Tuesday evening

Guggenheim — Each Tuesday evening

Made possible by grants from Mobil

Temple of Dendur at The Met — Thursday evenings Sept 28–Nov 16

The Masterworks of **Edvard Munch**

The Museum of Modern Art New York March 15–April 24, 1979

Presented with the support of Mobil Corporation and drawn from an exhibition organized by the National Gallery of Art, Washington

Mobil

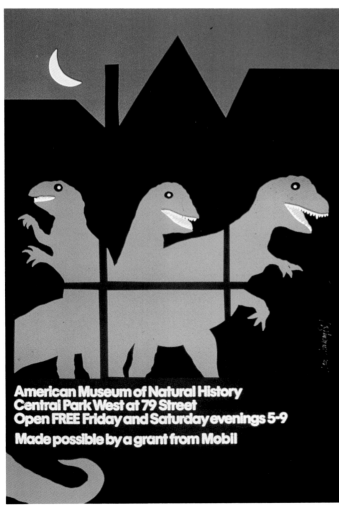

American Museum of Natural History Central Park West at 79 Street Open FREE Friday and Saturday evenings 5–9

Made possible by a grant from Mobil

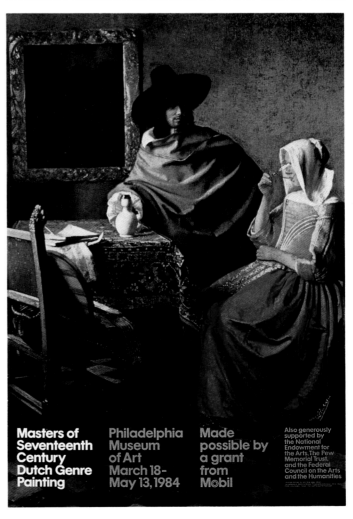

Masters of Seventeenth Century Dutch Genre Painting

Philadelphia Museum of Art March 18– May 13, 1984

Made possible by a grant from Mobil

Also generously supported by the National Endowment for the Arts, The Pew Memorial Trust, and the Federal Council on the Arts and the Humanities

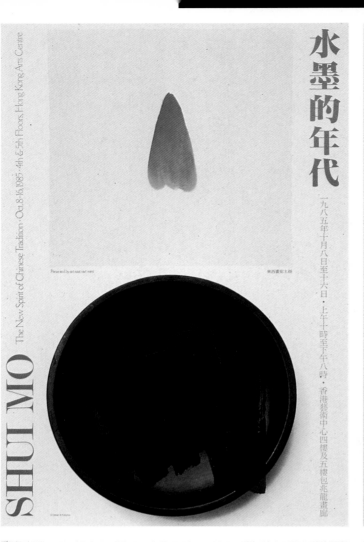

水墨的年代

SHUI MO

The New Spirit of Chinese Tradition · Oct. 8-16, 1985 · 4th & 5th Floors, Hong Kong Arts Centre

一九八五年十月八日至十六日 · 上午十時至下午八時 · 香港藝術中心四樓及五樓包兆龍畫廊

東西畫廊主辦

世界環境日：美的回響 香港著名畫家作品展

World Environment Day:
Artists' Responses
A Painting Exhibition by
Hong Kong Major Artists

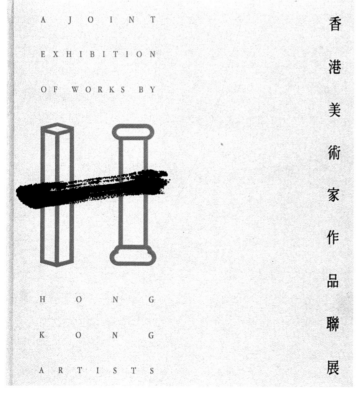

A JOINT
EXHIBITION
OF WORKS BY

HONG
KONG
ARTISTS

香港美術家作品聯展

一畫會會展

ONE ART GROUP SHOW

香港藝術中心四樓包兆龍畫廊

一九八二年二月廿二日至廿八日

PAO SUI LOONG GALLERIES

HONG KONG ARTS CENTRE

22-28 FEBRUARY 1981

DESIGN: KAN TAI-KEUNG

NEUE GALERIE FÜR HAMBURG

GALERIE
ART EAST
ART WEST

MODERNE CHINESISCHE KUNST
AUS HONG KONG

19. MAI — 30. JUNI 1988

Öffnungszeiten: Di, Do, Fr 11-18, Mi 11-20, Sa 11-14 Grindelallee 100, 2000 Hamburg 13, Tel: 040 — 45 77 25/65

Designer
Kan Tai-keung
Design Firm
Kan Tai-keung Design &
Associates Ltd., Hong Kong
Client
Galerie Art East/Art West

*"The new spirit of Chinese
tradition"*

Designer
Kan Tai-keung
Design Firm
Kan Tai-keung Design &
Associates Ltd., Hong Kong
Illustrator
Yam Chun Hon
Photographer
C. K. Wong
Client
WED Hong Kong Working Group

*"World Environment Day artists'
responses"*

Designer
Kan Tai-keung
Design Firm
Kan Tai-keung Design &
Associates Ltd., Hong Kong
Client
The Regional Council

*A joint exhibition of works by
Hong Kong artists*

Designer
Kan Tai-keung
Design Firm
Kan Tai-keung Design &
Associates Ltd., Hong Kong
Client
One Art Group

Designer
Kan Tai-keung
Design Firm
Kan Tai-keung Design &
Associates Ltd., Hong Kong
Client
Galerie Art East/Art West

*Modern Chinese art from
Hong Kong*

Designer
Pierre Mendell
Design Firm
Mendell & Oberer, Munich,
Germany
Client
Die Neue Pinakothek

*Poster for the opening of the
Neue Pinakothek, Munich.
(Translation) Visit us at the Neue
Pinakothek*

Designer
Steven Joseph
Design Firm
Spatchurst Design Associates,
N.S.W., Australia
Client
Biennale of Sydney

*'Japan Week' program from the
1988 Biennale of Sydney*

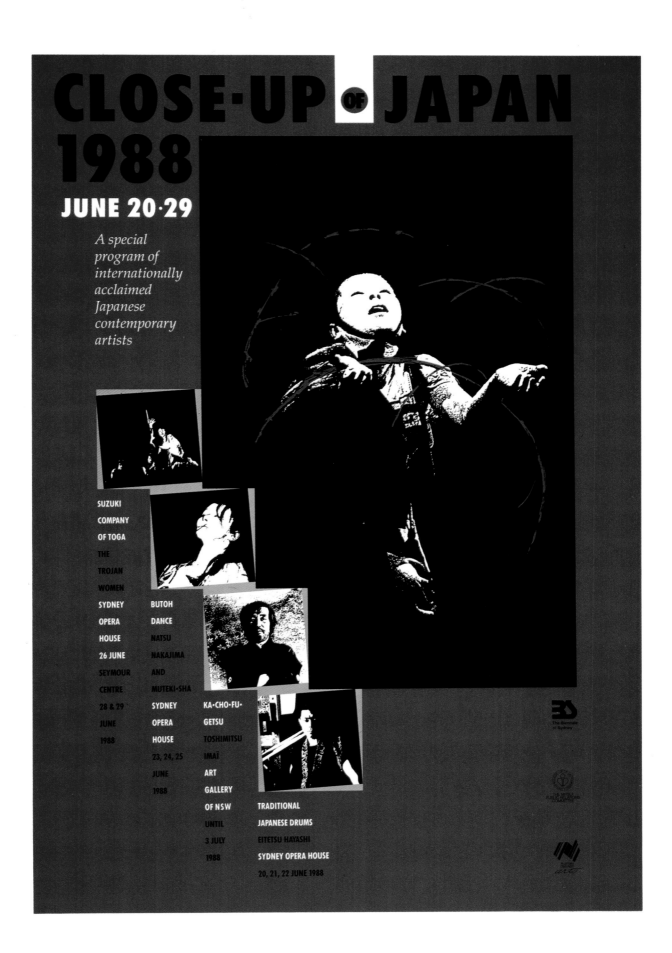

Designer/Illustrator
Seymour Chwast
Design Firm
The Pushpin Group Inc., New York

Client
Cia. Suzano de Papel & Celulose

Designer/Illustrator
Seymour Chwast

Design Firm
The Pushpin Group Inc.,
New York

Client
The Cooper Union

Designer/Illustrator
Seymour Chwast
Design Firm
The Pushpin Group Inc.,
New York
Client
IBM Gallery

Designer/Illustrator
Seymour Chwast
Design Firm
The Pushpin Group Inc.,
New York
Client
Lustrare Gallery

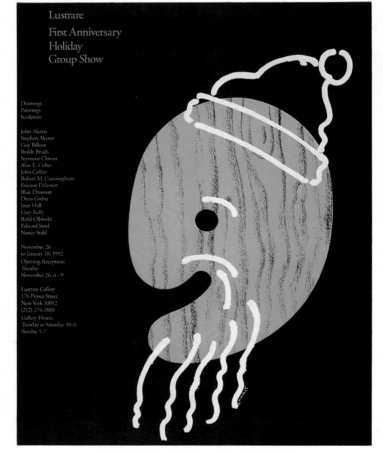

Designer
Marilyn Bouma-Pyper
Design Firm & Client
Art Gallery of Ontario, Canada
Illustrator
Gábor Bachman
Photographer
Imre Juhász
Copywriters
Roald Nasgaard, Clara Hargittay,
Aldona Satterthwaite

*Poster advertising exhibition of
contemporary Hungarian art,
probably one of the first
showings of post-communist art
in the western world.*

FREE WORLDS

Metaphors and Realities in Contemporary Hungarian Art

Art
Gallery
of
Ontario

18 October
1991 to
5 January
1992

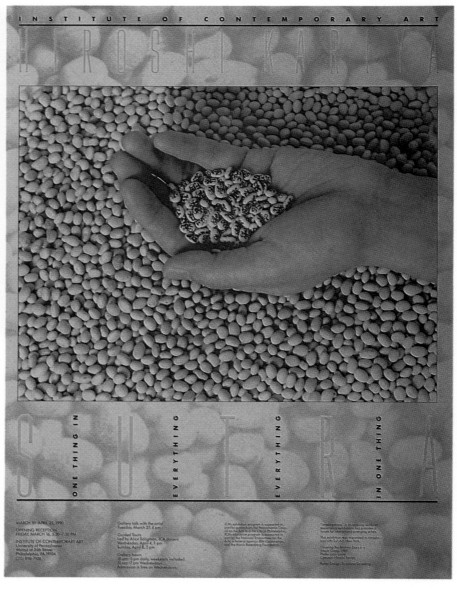

Designer
Lanny Sommese
Design Firm
Sommese Design, State College,
Pennsylvania
Client
Depree Art Center & Gallery

Designers
Joe Scorsone, Alice Drueding
Design Firm
Scorsone/Drueding, Jenkintown,
Pennsylvania
Photographer
Lary Lame
Copywriter
Julie Courtney
Client
Institute of Contemporary Art

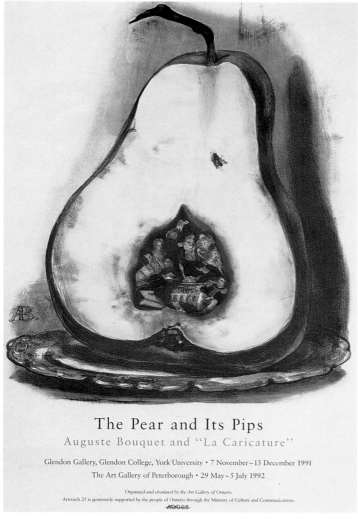

The Pear and Its Pips

Auguste Bouquet and "La Caricature"

Glendon Gallery, Glendon College, York University • 7 November–13 December 1991

The Art Gallery of Peterborough • 29 May–5 July 1992

Organized and circulated by the Art Gallery of Ontario
Artreach 25 is generously supported by the people of Ontario through the Ministry of Culture and Communications.

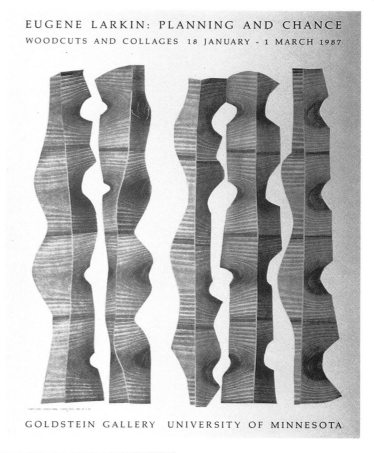

EUGENE LARKIN: PLANNING AND CHANCE

WOODCUTS AND COLLAGES 18 JANUARY - 1 MARCH 1987

GOLDSTEIN GALLERY UNIVERSITY OF MINNESOTA

Designer
Steven Boyle
Design Firm & Client
Art Gallery of Ontario, Canada

Poster reflects the larger than life aspect of the caricatures used to discredit King Louis-Philippe of France in the 1830s

RIKO DEBENJAK Razstava grafik ob 50. letnici avtorjeve prve razstave v
Ljubljani. Galerija Insula, Dvorni trg v Ljubljani, od 25. oktobra do 9. novembra 1990, od 10ᵸ-13ᵸ in od 16ᵸ-19ᵸ, v soboto in nedeljo zaprto.

Designer
Patrick M. Redmond
Design Firm
Design, Housing and Apparel
Graphic Design Studio,
University of Minnesota
Illustrator
Eugene Larkin
Client
Goldstein Gallery

Art Director/Designer
Edi Berk
Design Firm
KROG, Ljubljana, Slovenija
Copywriter
Brane Kovic
Client
Gallery INSULA, Ljubljana

Designers
Joe Scorsone, Alice Drueding
Design Firm
Scorsone/Drueding, Jenkintown,
Pennsylvania
Copywriter
Amy Orr
Client
Bucks County Community
College

Poster for exhibition on masks

Designer
Judy Kirpich
Design Firm
Grafik Communications Ltd.,
Alexandria, Virginia
Photographer
David Sharpe Inc.
Client
The Computer Museum

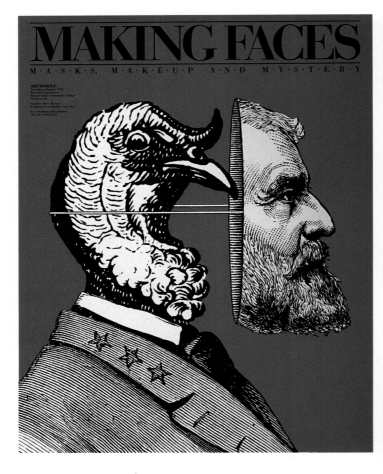

Designer/Illustrator
John Sayles
Design Firm
Sayles Graphic Design,
Des Moines, Iowa
Copywriter
Lore Solo
Client
State Historical Society of Iowa

*"The Delicate Balance" is a
permanent exhibit at the
historical museum in Des Moines.
The exhibit deals with man's
impact on his environment.*

THE DELICATE BALANCE

"HUMAN VALUES AND IOWA'S NATURAL RESOURCES" STATE HISTORICAL BUILDING DES MOINES, IOWA

BRAVE FORTUNE:

HEROIC IMAGES OF AMERICAN ENTERPRISE, 1930 - 1945

FASHION INSTITUTE OF TECHNOLOGY, JUNE 18 - AUGUST 3, 1991

TUESDAY - FRIDAY, 12:00 NOON - 8:00 P.M.; SATURDAY, 10:00 A.M. - 5:00 P.M.

COVER ART BY ANTONIO PETRUCCELLI JUNE 1937 ©1937 TIME INC. / POSTER DESIGN BY M PLUS M INCORPORATED, NY

Designer
Takaaki Matsumoto
Design Firm
M Plus M Incorporated,
New York
Client
Fashion Institute of Technology

Designer
Ann Wassman Gross
Design Firm & Client
Art Institute of Chicago, Illinois

Designer
Phil Conroy
Design Firm
Design North, Leeds, England
Illustrator
Hanife Hassan O'Keefe
Client
Cultural Resource Management

*Poster for The Jorvik Viking
Centre built on the site of an
original 10th century Viking
village founded in York, England.*

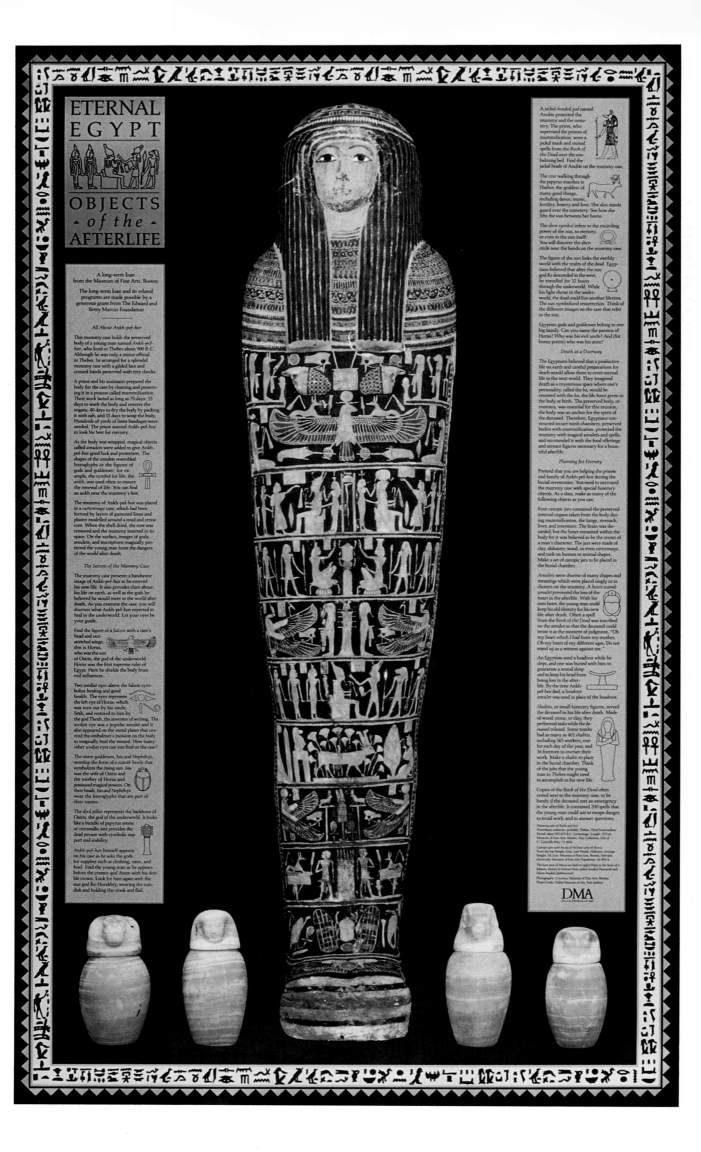

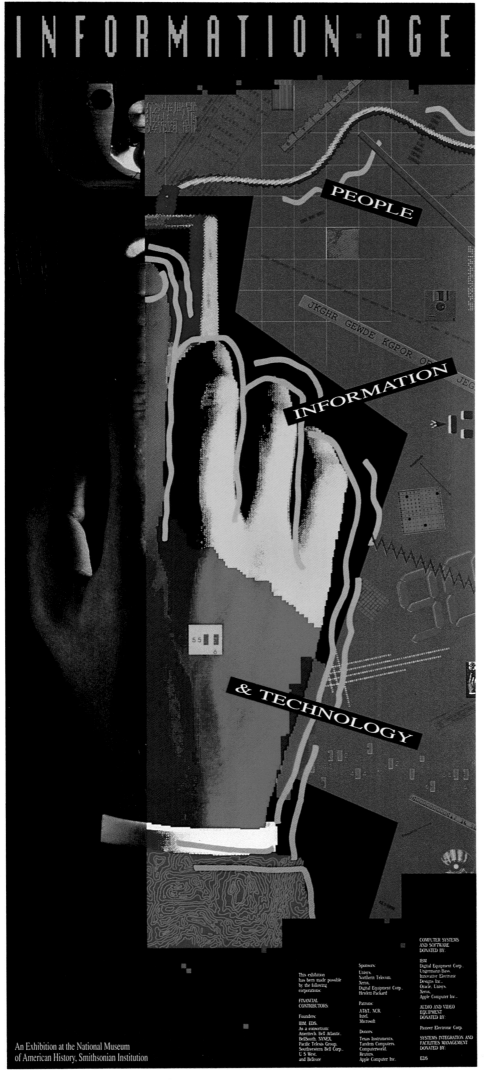

INFORMATION·AGE

PEOPLE

INFORMATION

& TECHNOLOGY

An Exhibition at the National Museum
of American History, Smithsonian Institution

Creative/Art Directors
Bob Rozelle, Greg Dittmar
Designer
Greg Dittmar
Design Firm & Client
Dallas Museum of Art,
Dallas, Texas
Illustrator
Greg Dittmar
Photographer
Tom Jenkins
Copywriters
Gail Davitt, Molly Gwinn

*Poster for exhibition sent out to
schools to use as teaching aid
before bringing classes to exhibit*

Designers
Melanie Bass, Gregg Glaviano,
Jennifer Johnson, Judy Kirpich
Design Firm
Grafik Communications Ltd.,
Alexandria, Virginia
Photographer
Joel Freid
Client
National Museum of American
History, Smithsonian Institution

Designer
André Toet
Design Firm
Samenwerkende Ontwerpers bv,
The Netherlands
Photographer
Maarten van de Velde
Copywriter
John Duivesteijn
Client
Volksbuurtmuseum (Working
Class Quarter Museum)

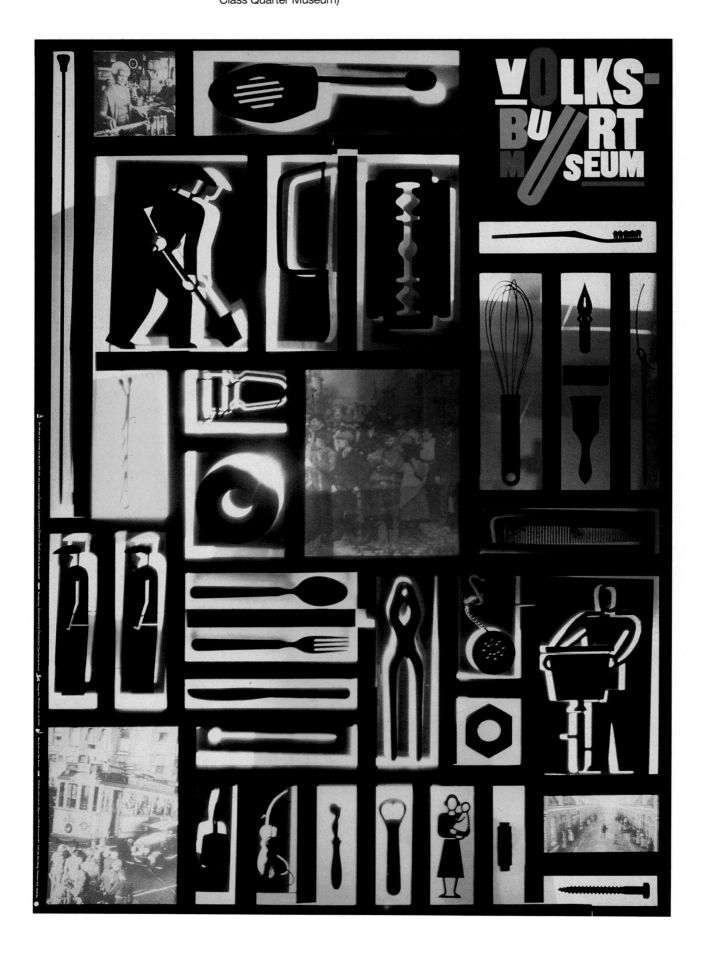

Designers
Joe Scorsone, Alice Drueding
Design Firm
Scorsone/Drueding,
Jenkintown, Pennsylvania
Copywriter
Judith Tannenbaum
Client
Institute of Contemporary Art

*Exhibition announcement/
invitation*

**INSTITUTE
OF
CONTEMPORARY
ART
UNIVERSITY
OF
PENNSYLVANIA**
PRESENTS
"FESTA CON SCANGA"

IMMEDIATELY FOLLOWING THE
ITALO SCANGA OPENING
WEDNESDAY, DECEMBER 10, 1986
OPENING 5–7 P.M.
"FESTA CON SCANGA" 7–11 P.M.
ICA GALLERIES
34TH & WALNUT STREETS
$30 PER PERSON
CHAIRMEN:
MR. AND MRS. RAMON R. NAUS

Designers
Joe Scorsone, Alice Drueding
Design Firm
Scorsone/Drueding,
Jenkintown, Pennsylvania
Illustrators
Joe Scorsone, Alice Drueding
Copywriter
Linda Milanesi
Client
James A. Michener Art Museum

Invitation to costume gala

JAMES A. MICHENER ART MUSEUM MASKED BALL GALA

The Board of Trustees and the Director of the James A. Michener Art Museum
cordially invite you to attend our Annual Gala on Saturday, September 14, 1991, 6 pm
138 South Pine Street, Doylestown, Pennsylvania

Mr. and Mrs. Albert Renzi, Gala Co-Chairpersons

Black Tie — RSVP — Couvert $125 per person / $1,250 per table

Designers
Joe Scorsone, Alice Drueding
Design Firm
Scorsone/Drueding,
Jenkintown, Pennsylvania
Copywriter
Judith Tannenbaum
Client
Institute of Contemporary Art

*Brochure announcing
symposium on arts in the 90's*

Creative/Art Directors
Michael McGinn, Takaaki
Matsumoto
Designer
Michael McGinn
Design Firm
M Plus M Incorporated,
New York
Client
Independent Curators
Incorporated

*Studio events announcement/
invitation*

Designer
Ann Wassmann Gross
Design Firm & Client
The Art Institute of Chicago,
Illinois

*Opening invitations for renovated
modern art galleries*

Creative/Art Directors
Michael McGinn, Takaaki
Matsumoto
Designer
Michael McGinn
Design Firm
M Plus M Incorporated,
New York
Client
Independent Curators
Incorporated

*Studio events announcement/
invitation*

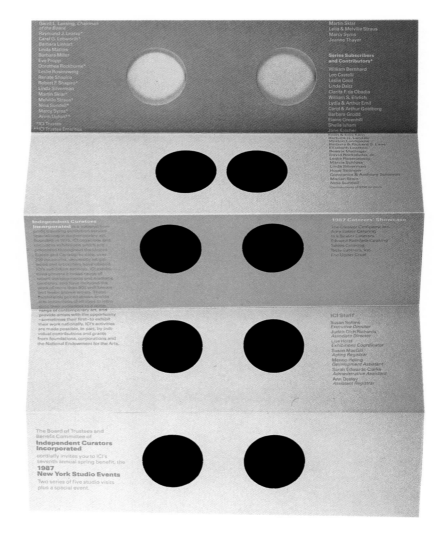

Designer
Alison Lackey
Design Firm
North Carolina Museum of Art,
Raleigh
Copywriter
Patrick McCusker

Invitation for member's event

Art Director/Illustrator
Lanny Sommese
Designer
Kristin Breslin
Design Firm
Sommese Design, State College,
Pennsylvania
Client
Zoller Gallery, School of Visual
Arts, Pennsylvania

*Brochure was sent out folded.
Blade of 'Exacto' was die cut so
as to act as closure. In order to
open brochure, 'Exacto' blade
had to be pulled out of eye.*

Designer
Joyce Nesnadny
Design Firm
Nesnadny & Schwartz,
Cleveland, Ohio
Photographers
Lorna Simpson, Nesnadny &
Schwartz
Client
The Progressive Corporation

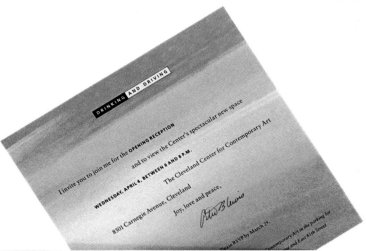

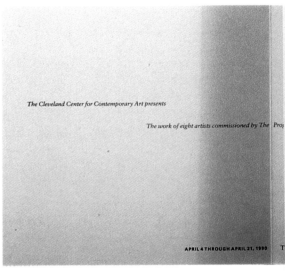

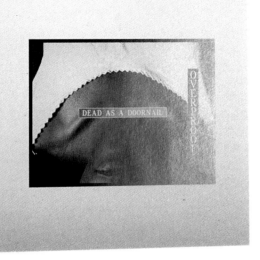

Designer
Lisa MacCollum
Design Firm & Client
The Heard Museum, Phoenix,
Arizona
Copywriter
Diana Pardue

Designer
David Ortega
Design Firm & Client
The Heard Museum, Phoenix,
Arizona
Photographer
Craig Smith
Copywriter
Diana Pardue

Exhibition invitation

COMPOSITION

FRANK LLOYD WRIGHT®

VISION

Inside left to right:
Urn, sheet copper, c. 1902, 19 × 19 × 19 inches.
Designed for the Susan Lawrence Dana house, Springfield, Illinois.
Settle, oak, with leather-covered seat cushion, c. 1912, 30½ × 80 × 32½ inches.
Designed for the William B. Greene house, Aurora, Illinois.
Three Luxfer Prisms, molded glass, patented October 4, 1897, each block 4 × 4 inches.
Designed for the American Luxfer Prism Company, Chicago, Illinois.

The exhibition is made possible by a generous grant from Domino's Pizza, Inc.
It was organized by the Smithsonian Institution Traveling Exhibition Service in
cooperation with the Domino's Center for Architecture & Design, Ann Arbor, Michigan.
The exhibition is presented in Dallas as one of the Chilton Exhibition Series.

"The square with FRANK LLOYD WRIGHT in block letters is a registered trademark
belonging to the Frank Lloyd Wright Foundation. The Frank Lloyd Wright
Foundation grants permission for one time use to the Dallas Museum of Art
for this mark in its exhibition invitation."

Designer
Greg Dittmar
Design Firm & Client
Dallas Museum of Art, Texas

Exhibition invitation

The Trustees and Staff of the
Dallas Museum of Art
cordially invite you to the
Members' opening of the exhibition

Frank Lloyd Wright:
Preserving an Architectural Heritage.
Decorative Designs from
The Domino's Pizza Collection

Saturday, May 25, from 10 am to 4 pm
Saturday, May 25, from 6 to 9 pm
or Sunday, May 26, from 6 to 9 pm

Presentation of this invitation admits two at the
Ceremonial Entrance, Harwood and Flora.

An illustrated introduction to the exhibition
will be given at 7 and 7:30 in the Auditorium
both evenings.

The Gallery Buffet will be open for dinner.
Reservations are required; please phone
(214) 922-1260.

TEXTURE   STRUCTURE

CLEVELAND CENTER for CONTEMPORARY ART *invites you to*

LOOK

AGAIN

Designer
Joyce Nesnadny
Design Firm
Nesnadny & Schwartz,
Cleveland, Ohio
Copywriter
Cleveland Center for
Contemporary Art
Client
Cleveland Center for
Contemporary Art

Membership package

The Trustees and Staff

of the Dallas Museum of Art

cordially invite you to

the Members' opening

of the exhibitions

Court Arts of Indonesia and

Spirit and Place: Photographs

of Indonesia by John Gollings

Saturday, February 9, 10 am to 4 pm

Saturday, February 9, 6 to 9 pm

or Sunday, February 10, 6 to 9 pm

Presentation of this

invitation at the door admits two.

An illustrated introduction

to the exhibition

will be given at 7:30 in the

Auditorium both evenings.

Creative/Art Directors
Bob Rozelle, Greg Dittmar
Designer
Greg Dittmar
Design Firm & Client
Dallas Museum of Art, Texas
Photographer
Tom Jenkins

Exhibition invitation

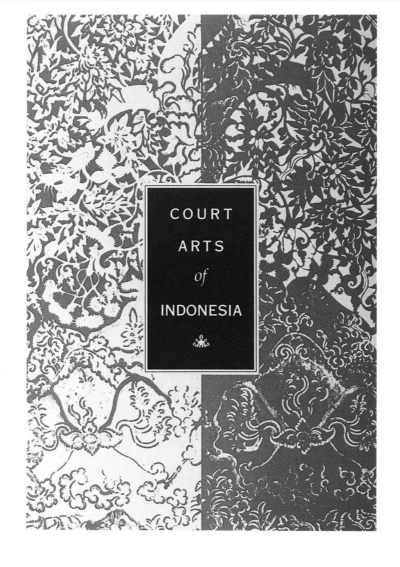

COURT

ARTS

of

INDONESIA

Creative/Art Directors
Meg Wilson, Greg Dittmar
Designer
Greg Dittmar
Design Firm & Client
Dallas Museum of Art, Texas
Illustrator
Russell Sublette
Copywriter
Carolyn Tate

Gallery guide

GUIDE TO THE
PRE-COLUMBIAN
GALLERY

GUIA DE LA GALERIA
PRECOLOMBINA

Come see stuff even older than your parents.

We're talking ancient. Like Indian headdresses and arrowheads. Fossils and skeletons. And a bunch of other fun stuff to see and do. It's on June 15, from 9 AM to 5 PM, at the Museum of Natural History at Roger Williams Park. There's a free reggae concert featuring Luko Adjaffi and One Nation, from 3 PM to 5 PM. If you want to know anything more, call 785-9451. And after this, you'll never call him your old man again.

Museum Membership Day

Come teach your kids about the birds and the bees.

Teach them about the facts of wildlife at the Museum of Natural History's Membership Day. There will be a bird walk, an insect scavenger hunt, and a bunch of other fun stuff to see and do. June 15, from 9 AM to 5 PM, the Museum of Natural History at Roger Williams Park. Free reggae concert featuring Luko Adjaffi and One Nation, from 3 PM to 5 PM. For more information, call 785-9451. Don't let them learn this stuff on the street.

Museum Membership Day

Introduce your Kids to the beetles and the stones.

Start up your weekend at the Museum of Natural History's Membership Day. There will be a rock identification table (bring a rock and we'll tell you what it is), an insect scavenger hunt, and a bunch of other fun stuff to see and do. June 15, from 9 AM to 5 PM, the Museum of Natural History at Roger Williams Park. Free reggae concert featuring Luko Adjaffi and One Nation, from 3 PM to 5 PM. For more information, call 785-9451. All you need is to love learning with your kids. Yeah, yeah, yeah!

Museum Membership Day

Art Director/Designer
Bobbie Friedman
Design Firm
PotterHazlehurst Inc.,
E. Greenwich, Rhode Island
Copywriter
Spencer Deadrick
Client
Museum of Natural History,
Roger Williams Park

The Museum of Natural History at Roger Williams Park is definitely not the stuffy place you visited on third-grade field trips. And this party was definitely not the type of affair one would normally associate with a museum. To give it a somewhat rowdy flavour, we named the party "ClamJam '91." We took nineteenth-century naturalist illustrations and dressed them up for the party. We then added hand-drawn borders and headlines. A great time was had by all.

Art Director/Designer
Allen McDavid Stoddard
Design Firm
Allen McDavid Stoddard,
Spartanburg, S. Carolina
Illustrator/Copywriter
Allen McDavid Stoddard
Client
Converse College

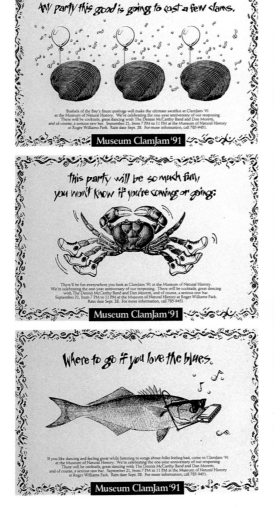

Any party this good is going to cost a few clams.

Bushels of the Bay's finest quahogs will make the ultimate sacrifice at ClamJam '91 at the Museum of Natural History. We're celebrating the one-year anniversary of our reopening. There will be cocktails, great dancing with The Dennis McCarthy Band and Dan Moretti, and of course, a serious raw bar. September 21, from 7 PM to 11 PM at the Museum of Natural History at Roger Williams Park. Rain date Sept. 28. For more information, call 785-9451.

Museum ClamJam '91

this party will be so much fun, you won't know if you're coming or going.

There'll be fun everywhere you look at ClamJam '91 at the Museum of Natural History. We're celebrating the one-year anniversary of our reopening. There will be cocktails, great dancing with The Dennis McCarthy Band and Dan Moretti, and of course, a serious raw bar. September 21, from 7 PM to 11 PM at the Museum of Natural History at Roger Williams Park. Rain date Sept. 28. For more information, call 785-9451.

Museum ClamJam '91

Where to go if you love the blues.

If you like dancing and feeling great while listening to songs about folks feeling bad, come to ClamJam '91 at the Museum of Natural History. We're celebrating the one-year anniversary of our reopening. There will be cocktails, great dancing with The Dennis McCarthy Band and Dan Moretti, and of course, a serious raw bar. September 21, from 7 PM to 11 PM at the Museum of Natural History at Roger Williams Park. Rain date Sept. 28. For more information, call 785-9451.

Museum ClamJam '91

The Faculty
mac boggs
judy jones
teresa prater
frazer pajak
david zacharias
marc yops

exhibits:
DECEMBER 3-24
MILLIKEN GALLERY
CONVERSE COLLEGE
SPARTANBURG, SC

Designer/Illustrator
Paul Asao
Design Firm
Earle Palmer Brown, Tampa,
Florida
Copywriter
Patrick Hanlon
Client
The Salvador Dali Museum

*Billboard for the Salvador Dali
Museum in St. Petersburg,
Florida*

THE WIDEST COLLECTION OF DALI ART IN THE WORLD.

SALVADOR DALI MUSEUM
St. Petersburg

Red Haring.
Keith Haring. Tampa Museum of Art. June 16–Sept 1.

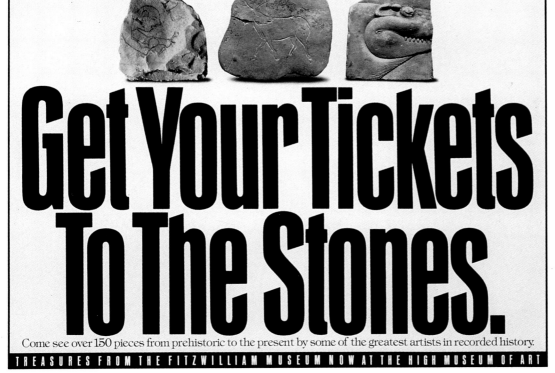

Get Your Tickets To The Stones.

Come see over 150 pieces from prehistoric to the present by some of the greatest artists in recorded history.

TREASURES FROM THE FITZWILLIAM MUSEUM NOW AT THE HIGH MUSEUM OF ART

Designer
David Hodges
Design Firm
Earle Palmer Brown, Tampa,
Florida
Illustrator
Keith Haring
Copywriter
Patrick Hanlon
Client
The Tampa Museum of Art

*Keith Haring, one of America's
most popular modern pop
artists, famous for his "graffiti"
art, was having a showing of his
work at the Tampa Museum of
Art in Tampa, Florida.*

Designer
Joe Paprocki
Design Firm
Earle Palmer Brown, Tampa,
Florida
Copywriter
Patrick Hanlon
Client
The High Museum, Atlanta

*The High Museum of Art in
Atlanta took advantage of the
Rolling Stones rock group
national concert tour to promote
a new exhibition.*

Designers
Randall Leers, Laura McCurdy
Design Firm
LMC Design, Burlington,
Vermont
Photographer
Ken Burris
Copywriter
Shelburne Museum
Client
Shelburne Museum

Brochure

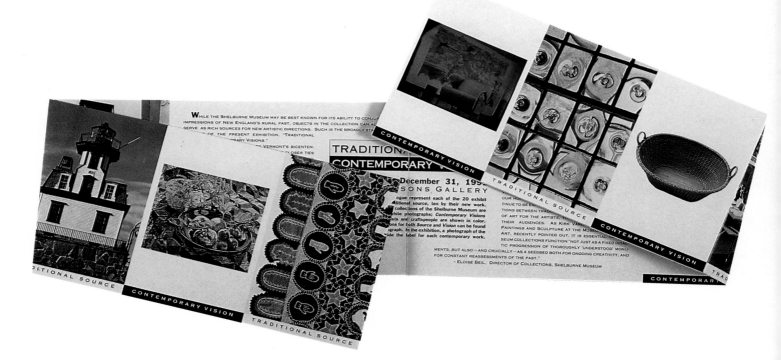

Publications Director
Nicole F. Gorak
Design Firm & Client
University Art Museum,
California State University,
Long Beach

Gallery handout

125 Years of Musical Theater
IBM Gallery of Science and Art May 14 – July 13, 1991
An exhibition organized by the Museum of the City of New York

BROADWAY!

Designer
Seymour Chwast
Design Firm
The Pushpin Group Inc.,
New York
Illustrator
Seymour Chwast
Client
IBM Gallery

Poster & brochure

No similar exhibition has been made in an American stage," wrote a *New York Times* critic on September 13, 1866, the morning after *The Black Crook* premiered at Niblo's Garden on Broadway. First night audiences had both treated to scantily clad women, breathtaking scenery and stunning special effects. *The Black Crook*—generally acknowledged to be the first Broadway musical—contained no uniquely American theatrical innovations. Instead, it borrowed from the music hall, burlesque, grand opera and popular spectacle, all of which had their origins in Europe. But the one indigenous entertainment form that would strongly influence American musical theater—the minstrel show—had already begun to be seen in Broadway theaters.

Since the opening of *The Black Crook* about

125 years ago, the Broadway musical has evolved, at times dramatically, by incorporating changes in taste and technology, and has continually mirrored the political and social climate of the times. But the musical's primary mission has always been, as it was at Niblo's, to entertain. *Broadway! 125 Years of Musical Theater* offers a look at that entertainment and the stories, songs, dances and stars that have given it life.

Thirteen years after *The Black Crook*, Ned Harrigan and Tony Hart's series of plays about the fictitious Mulligan Guards first offered farcical stories about the struggles of immigrants to adapt to a new way of life, and the Broadway musical began to address distinctively American themes. African-American music was introduced to Broadway at the turn of the century in shows such as *A Trip to Coontown* (1898), the first musical

written, produced and performed by African-Americans, and *In Dahomey* (1903), starring Bert Williams and George Walker. These early shows offered syncopated rhythms from vaudeville and minstrel shows that would profoundly shape later American musical scores.

In the early years of the twentieth century, Broadway was marked by George M. Cohan's uniquely patriotic *Little Johnny Jones* (1904), which reiterated the decades-old theme that the American personality was far superior to the European in both morals and manners. Later in the decade, however, Franz Lehár's European operetta *The Merry Widow* (1907) caught the imagination of Americans with the beauty of its waltzes and the sheer romanticism of its story. The subsequent success of German and Austrian operettas represented a dependence on foreign musical conven-

tions, but it also set the stage for the emphasis on melody that would characterize both later American operetta and the work of composers such as Rodgers and Hammerstein.

The popularity of European operetta faded with the wave of anti-German sentiment during World War I. Meanwhile, young American composers such as Irving Berlin and Jerome Kern had begun to shape a distinctly American musical idiom. In *Watch Your Step* (1914), for example, Berlin popularized ragtime rhythms, borrowed from African-American music, that delighted Americans and spurred on a new dance craze personified by the revue's glamorous stars, Vernon and Irene Castle. Kern's Princess Theater musicals (1915–18) combined ragtime with ballads to create danceable scores with lighthearted, believable stories. Together the Princess shows led the way toward a

truly American musical comedy.

During the same period, Florenz Ziegfeld's annual *Follies* (1907–1931) had begun to elevate the revue format to new heights of achievement. Joseph Urban's lavish settings, the music of Kern, Berlin and Victor Herbert, and some of the world's most glamorous showgirls provided Ziegfeld with glittering backgrounds for an array of talented performers that included Will Rogers, W. C. Fields, Fanny Brice, Bert Williams and Marilyn Miller. The Twenties witnessed George and Ira Gershwin's first complete show, *Lady Be Good* (1924), as well as a strong resurgence of operetta, with productions such as Rudolf Friml's *Rose Marie* and Sigmund Romberg's *The Student Prince* (both 1924).

Perhaps the greatest musical theater achievement of the decade was *Show Boat* (1927), by Je-

rome Kern and Oscar Hammerstein II. The show's score represented a unique blend of jazz and operetta, and the story interwove a serious tale of lovers separated and crushed by racial segregation with a more traditional account of an innocent young woman's marriage to a gambler. Although it borrowed from earlier musical forms, *Show Boat* departed sharply from its predecessors on the Broadway musical stage by more fully integrating its score and book, prompting many critics to call it a genuine American masterpiece.

With the Stock Market crash of 1929 and competition from the new sound films developed at the end of the Twenties, Broadway musicals became smaller and less costly. During the 1930s, the number of new musical productions dropped by twenty percent, and the extravaganzas of the previous decade largely disappeared. But some traditional

BROADWAY!

**125 YEARS OF
MUSICAL THEATER**
IBM GALLERY OF SCIENCE AND ART
MAY 14–JULY 13, 1991

Art Director
Lisa Naffolin
Designers
Lisa Naffolin, Sunil Bhandari
(Harris Bhandari Design Assoc.)
Design Firm & Client
Art Gallery of Ontario, Canada
Photographer
Carlos Catenazzi

*Poster designed to support the
exhibition INDIVIDUALITÉS: 14
contemporary artists from France
at the Art Gallery of Ontario.*

AGO
film

Richard Hancox

AGO
film

Ulrike Ottinger

EXHIBITIONS

WORKSHOPS

"ARTISTS WITH THEIR WORK"

AGO

EXTENSION SERVICES

Art Gallery of Ontario
317 Dundas Street West
Toronto, Ontario
Canada M5T 1G4

Art Director/Designer
Steven Boyle
Design Firm & Client
Art Gallery of Ontario, Canada

"Artists With Their Work". This program offered through the Art Gallery of Ontario's Extension Services department features a broad range of artists working in various different mediums, who will give talks and demonstrations out in the community.

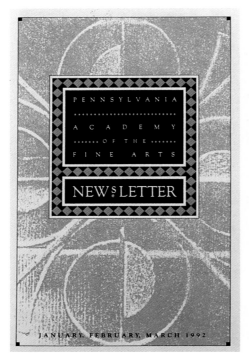

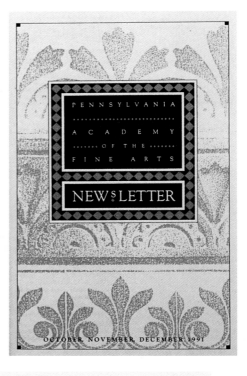

JANUARY, FEBRUARY, MARCH 1992

JULY, AUGUST, SEPTEMBER 1991

OCTOBER, NOVEMBER, DECEMBER 1991

Designers
Joe Scorsone, Alice Drueding
Design Firm
Scorsone/Drueding, Jenkintown,
Pennsylvania
Copywriter
Sharon Skeel
Client
Pennsylvania Academy of the
Fine Arts

Newsletters

Art Director
Lisa MacCollum
Designer
David Ortega
Design Firm & Client
The Heard Museum, Phoenix, Arizona
Illustrator
Lisa MacCollum
Copywriter
Mary Brennan

Quarterly calendar

The Heard Museum Calendar

September/October/November *1991*

Events

Members Only!
MEMBERS ARE INVITED to a special reception for **KAY WALKINGSTICK: EPHEMERAL/ETERNAL** Friday, Sept. 6, 6:30 to 8:30 p.m. Meet WalkingStick, who will give a brief talk at 7 p.m. on the evolution of her work. The reception also celebrates the recent opening of **INSPIRED BY SONG: SELECTIONS FROM THE DENMAN COLLECTION**. Bring your Membership Card or Invitation for admission.

EXCLUSIVE MEMBERS ONLY PREVIEW RECEPTION Friday, Oct. 18, 6:30 to 8:30 p.m. for **BEHIND THE MASK IN MEXICO.** Experience this extraordinary exhibit highlighting six masked Mexican festivals; shop at the Guild mercado, stocked with a variety of Dia de los Muertos (Day of the Dead) craft items; and view an authentic Dia de los Muertos altar in the Central Courtyard. Bring your Membership Card or Invitation for admission.

THIS FALL, GET ACQUAINTED with unique art forms and the artists who create them. **SPECIAL WEEKEND DEMONSTRATIONS** at the Museum are made possible by the De Grazia Art and Cultural Foundation, Tucson. Demonstrations are free with Museum admission and are held during regular Museum hours.
Sept. 14-15: Fern Sluder (Kiowa), ribbon work
Oct. 5-6: Bernice Monte (Tohono O'odham), baskets
Oct. 26-27: Jose and Hilario Quezado, Casas Grandes pottery

MEXICAN FOLK TRADITIONS – Authority Linda McAllister makes two presentations in October. The free talks, sponsored by the Arizona Humanities Council, are Wednesdays, 6:45-7:45 p.m.
Oct. 2: "Fireworks, Flowers, and Incense: The Mexican Festival Cycle"
Oct. 16: "From the Altar to the Cemetery: An Introduction to Dia de los Muertos"

DIA DE LOS MUERTOS FESTIVAL
Saturday, Oct. 19,10 a.m.-6 p.m. – Join us for parades led by the skeleton puppet, Dona Sebastiana, lots of hands-on art activities, non-stop Hispanic entertainment, fully-stocked Guild mercado, delicious, south-of-the-border food, and a candlelight closing procession. Museum admission includes both Museum and Festival – Members receive an exclusive 50% admission discount.

NATIVE AMERICAN PERFORMERS – dancers, musicians, and singers – pay tribute to our country's military veterans at the Museum's **ANNUAL GOURD DANCE,** Nov. 3. The free event is in the Amphitheater, noon-4 p.m. Delicious frybread will be for sale.

THANKSGIVING WEEKEND AT THE HEARD Nov. 29-Dec.1. Traditional Native American dancers, contemporary Native American musicians, and South American musicians will entertain (see schedule under performances). **Special Weekend Demonstrations! PLUS FRYBREAD!** for sale from 11 a.m. to 3 p.m. Friday and Saturday; noon-4 p.m. Sunday in the Auditorium.

Performances

Join us weekends for 20-30 minute performances by talented Native American and other ethnic entertainers; free with Museum admission.

Saturdays, 11 a.m. and 1:00 p.m.
Sundays at 2:30 p.m.

September
1 Tree Cody (Maricopa/Dakota), flute music

7 Little Soldiers Dance Group, Plains Indian dances
8 Carmen and Zarco, Brazilian music

14 Nostros, Latin American folk music
15 Robert Ameelyenah (Cocopah), Mohave bird songs

21 Yellow Bird Indian Dancers, Plains Indian dances
22 Keith Secola (Ojibwa) & the Echo contemporary Native American M

28 Delphine Tsinajinnie (Navaj
29 Brent Michael Davids (Stockb Mohegan), contemporary Native Ame music

October
5 Moontie Sinquah (Hopi/Choctaw) & Vincent Davis (Hopi/Choctaw), Grass Dance & Fancy Dance
6 Moontie Sinquah (Hopi/Choctaw) & Vincent Davis (Hopi/Choctaw), Grass Dance & Fancy Dance

12 Little Soldiers Dance Group, Plains Indian dances
13 Carmen & Zarco, Latin American music

19 DIA DE LOS MUERTOS FESTIVAL, 10 a.m.-6 p.m.
20 David A. Montour (Delaware), flute music

26 Yaqui Deer Dance Group
27 Keith Secola (Ojibwa) & The EchoMakers, contemporary Native American music

November
2 Moontie Sinquah (Hopi/Choctaw) & Vincent Davis (Hopi/Choctaw), Grass Dance & Fancy Dance
3 GOURD DANCE, noon-4 p.m.

9 Delphine Tsinajinnie (Navajo), singer
10 David A. Montour (Delaware), flute music

16 Keith Secola (Ojibwa) & The EchoMakers, contemporary Native American Music
17 Robert Ameelyenah (Cocopah), Mohave bird songs

23 Yaqui Deer Dance Group
24 Nosotros, Latin American folk music

THANKSGIVING WEEKEND
29 (11 a.m. & 1 p.m.) Yellow Bird Indian Dancers, Plains Indian dances.
30 (11 a.m. & 1 p.m.) Little Soldiers Dancers, Plains Indian dances
1 (Dec., 2:30 p.m.) Carmen & Zarco, Highland South American Music

Workshops

Enrollment is limited on a first-come, first-served basis. Pre-register to Education Department, (602) 252-8840, ext. 512. Refund of a registration fee can be made only if a cancellation is made at least five working days before the start of a workshop. Space limited to ten per workshop, eight for cooking workshop.

**CHIMAYO TEXT
SIUM,** Nov. 9-10
Irvin and Lisa
cased in **G
TIONS.**
"Desi

B
Sep
Beaded
Oct. 27
Beaded Ear
13 or Nov. 17
Making Frybread:
Nov. 13
Lazy Stitch Beading: O
Baking Mexican Bread (P
Oct. 23
Cooking Mexican Food (Mole):
Loom Beading: Nov. 20

AdultWorks

Beadwork
Several beading techniques taught by accomplished artists Daisy Simms (Quechan) and Yolanda Stevens (Cocopah/Quechan)
Sept. 14, 21 & 28;
9 a.m.-noon
Fee includes materials:
$36 Member; $45 Public

Navajo Cast Jewelry
Silver casting using traditional Navajo methods taught by silversmith Monica King (Navajo/Pima)
Nov. 16 & 23, 9 a.m.-4:30 p.m.
Fee includes materials and lunch:
$120 Member; $150 Public

The Heard Museum
22 East Monte Vista Road
Phoenix, Arizona 85004-1480

Amuse months
The Heard Museum Calendar

Creative/Art Directors
Jane Weeks, John Muller
Designer
Mike Regnier
Design Firm
Muller & Co., Kansas City,
Missouri
Photographer
David Marks
Client
Kansas City Art Institute

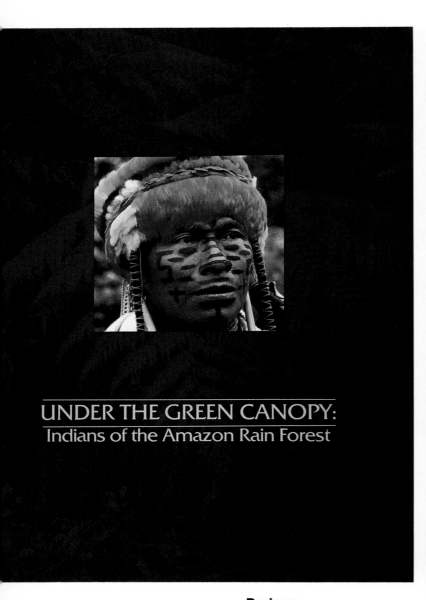

UNDER THE GREEN CANOPY:
Indians of the Amazon Rain Forest

Designer
Lisa MacCollum
Design Firm & Client
The Heard Museum, Phoenix,
Arizona
Photographers
Patrick Neary, Loren McIntyre
Copywriter
Diana Pardue

Exhibition invitation

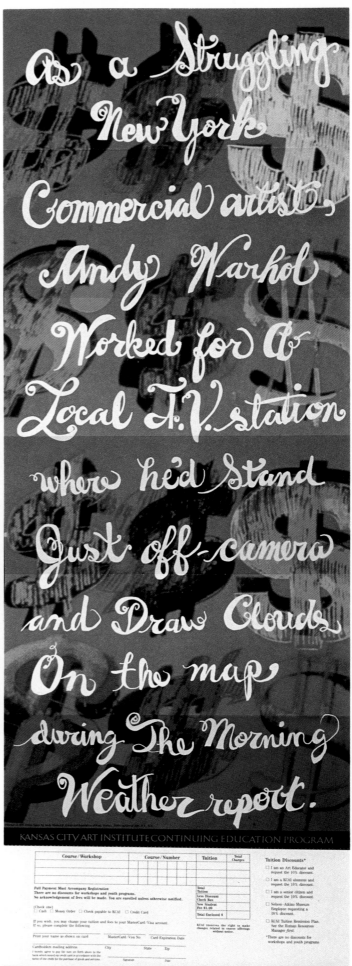

Publications Director
Nicole F. Gorak
Design Firm & Client
University Art Museum,
California State University,
Long Beach

Membership brochure

Cover: Sebastiano Ricci,
The Ecstasy of Saint Francis, c. 1693
(detail from A Collection Rediscovered)

how to join

MEMBER BENEFITS

FIVE LEVELS OF SUPPORT

Museum Associates, individuals who would like to become familiar with the many resources offered by the UAM, receive

• Special invitations to exhibitions, previews, private receptions, artists' lectures, and members-only events
• Opportunities to volunteer in the museum, or to become a docent
• The UAM newsletter
• A 10% discount at the Museum Shop
• One complimentary UAM publication
• Permit parking for special events

Active Members, an upgraded category of donors, receive these additional privileges:

• Tours to museums and galleries
• Two complimentary UAM publications
• A Museum Shop gift certificate

Sponsor Members, those community leaders who wish to make an additional commitment to the UAM and support educational programs receive these

additional privileges:

• A special event for sponsor members
• All catalogues and brochures published by the UAM
• Recognition on a plaque at the entrance to the museum

Contemporary Council Members, a select group of connoisseurs with a special interest in being active participants in the museum's many programs, assist with acquisitions and receive these additional privileges:

• Informal meetings with noted artists and collectors
• Year-round priority parking
• Private gallery talks
• Special previews
• Behind-the-scenes tours and travel

Benefactors/Corporate Members, who recognize visual arts education as a vital aspect of a quality university and want to make a contribution to ensure the continuation of the museum's many scholarly programs, receive these additional privileges:

• Complimentary tickets to all special events
• Opportunities for corporate events in the museum

Simply return your membership application in the attached envelope and you will become part of a growing community of people whose lives are enriched by the arts. You will belong to the first art museum on a public university campus in the greater Los Angeles area to be fully accredited by the American Association of Museums, which places the UAM in the top ten percent

of museums nationwide. The California Arts Council has ranked the museum among the top six art institutions in the state, calling it "a model for university museums." As a member of the UAM you will become our partner in assuring the ongoing vitality of the visual arts — in education, in Long Beach, and in Southern California.

The Museum Shop showcases UAM publications, art catalogues, and special gifts — from UAM logo totes and T-shirts to treasures by famous artists and designers. Members receive a 10% discount.

Parking reservations for guests visiting on weekdays may be made by calling 213/985-5761. Weekend parking is permitted in all ungated lots.

FOR INFORMATION
• **HOURS**
• **EXHIBITIONS**
• **EVENTS**
• **DIRECTIONS**
CALL 213/985-5761

**University Art Museum
California State University
Long Beach
1250 Bellflower Blvd.
5th Floor Library
Long Beach, CA 90840
213/985-5761**

From the 405, 605, or 22 West, exit 7th St. West; right on West Campus Dr.; right to parking circle and booth.

UAM ENTRANCE
5TH FLOOR

UNIVERSITY
ART
MUSEUM
An
Invitation
To
Discover

UAM

Order form

Name
Address
City
State
Zip
Phone

Please check one category:
☐ Museum Associate $30/CSULB Student ☐ Faculty ☐ Staff ☐ $15
☐ Museum Active $60
☐ Museum Sponsor $150
☐ Contemporary Council $300
☐ Benefactor/Corporate $500

This is a new membership ☐   This is a renewal ☐

Please send me further information about
Museum Docents ☐
Campus Council ☐

University Art Museum
California State University
Long Beach
1250 Bellflower Boulevard
Long Beach, CA 90840

For more information call
213/985-5761

Please charge to my VISA ☐ MASTERCARD ☐
My check is enclosed ☐
Signature
Card number
Expiration date

Lorna Simpson
Three Seated Figures, 1989
from Centric 38

Annette Messager
Les Broderies, 1989
(left to right) and John Richards
from UAM Studio Magazine Collection

Ettore Sottsass
New Art from Italy
installation photograph

The University
Art Museum
at California
State University
Long Beach
Located on the campus of one of California's largest and most prestigious universities, the University Art Museum embodies the fact that lifelong learning only begins in the classroom. The UAM is an integral part of CSULB's commitment to interdisciplinary understanding as well as academic and artistic excellence.

UAM

The Collections
The extensive holdings of the University Art Museum, primarily contemporary works of art on paper, are augmented by site-specific sculpture located throughout the campus, and known as "the museum without walls." Works from the collection are shown annually and are always available to scholars, while scheduled outdoor sculpture tours or informal picnics offer a popular introduction to the museum.

The Exhibitions
Through dynamic exhibitions that are both innovative and diverse, the UAM continues to introduce new work by some of the world's most celebrated contemporary artists, and reintroduces historic art in an informative and scholarly context. The UAM's pioneering Museum Studies Program, annual student exhibitions, and biannual faculty shows enhance the art experience of students and campus visitors alike, while the Centric series, an NEA supported program, provides opportunities to become acquainted with experimental art and artists not previously seen on the West Coast.

Bryan Hunt
Conductor II, 1983, Coll. UAM

Gabriela Ayarbide
Angel Woman, Señora Dorient
Mexico, 1979
from Centric 38

The Programs
Participating in the wide variety of programs that supplement exhibitions is one of the most rewarding aspects of UAM membership. The Zeitlin Lectures feature renowned artists, art historians, critics, architects, and educators. Noon in the Gallery is an informal forum that includes conversations with the artists; panel discussions devoted to timely, often controversial topics; and lectures that explore the world of art. The Docent Program also invites members to volunteer in the museum's many educational activities.

Jonathan Borofsky
I Dreamed Man at 2,841,789, 1983
from Focus on the Image

Chiyoko Arimoto
Candy, 1987
from Arimoto: Just Bronze

Museum Shop

University Art Museum
California State University, Long Beach
1250 Bellflower Boulevard
Long Beach, California 90840

Thank You
For Paying
The
Postage

Creative/Art Directors
John Muller, Jane Weeks
Design Firm
Muller & Co., Kansas City, Missouri
Photographer
John Krueger
Client
Kansas City Artist's Coalition

Art Director
Lanny Sommese
Designer
Carol Doremski
Design Firm
Sommese Design, State College, Pennsylvania
Client
Zoller Gallery, School of Visual Arts, Pennsylvania

Postcard for exhibition of work by School of Visual Arts faculty

Art Director
Nancy Ahrens
Designer
Alison Lackey
Design Firm
North Carolina Museum of Art,
Raleigh

Educational programs calendar

Art Director
Frédéric Metz
Designers
François Beauchamp,
André Gagnon
Design Firm & Client
Centre de Design de l'Université
du Québec, Canada
Illustrator/Photographer
Michel Brunelle, Roger Mazerolle
Copywriter
Jean-Yves Girard

Self promotion brochure

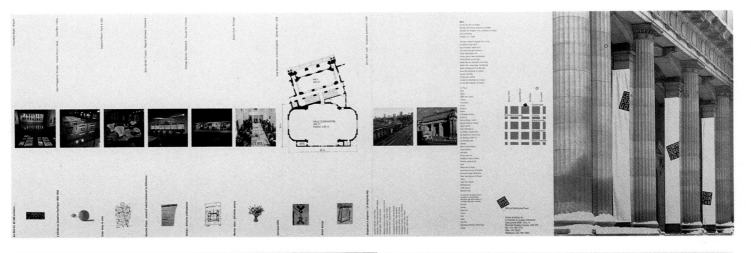

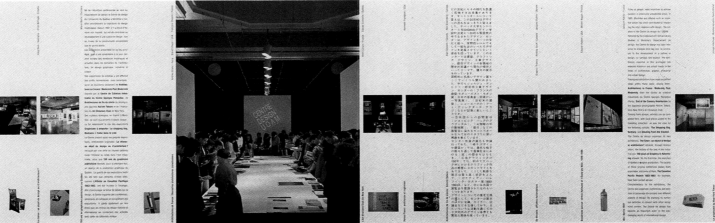

Art Director/Designer
Takaaki Matsumoto
Design Firm
M Plus M Incorporated,
New York
Client
Gallery 91

*Brochure entitled "91 Ways to
Destroy the World"*

91 Ways to Destroy	30. Fanaticism	61. Narcissism
the World	31. Fascism	62. Narrow mindedness
01. Aggression	32. Fashion victims	63. Neo-nazis
02. AIDS	33. Film colorization	64. Noise pollution
03. Alcoholism	34. Forgery	65. Nuclear disaster
04. Animal testing	35. Fraud	66. Nuclear weapons
05. Apartheid	36. Fundamentalism	67. Oil spills
06. Arson	37. Fur fashions	68. Plastic
07. Assault & Battery	38. Gangs	69. Poaching
08. Automatic weapons	39. Genetic engineering	70. Politics
09. Beauty pageants	40. Global warming	71. Pollution
10. Blackmail	41. Greed	72. Racism
11. Brain washing	42. Hate mongers	73. Rape
12. Bribery	43. Homelessness	74. Religion
13. Burglary	44. Homophobia	75. Repression
14. Capitalism	45. Ignorance	76. Robbery
15. Censorship	46. Incest	77. Sexism
16. Cheap champagne	47. Infomercials	78. Shortsightedness
17. Cheating	48. Insensitivity	79. Slavery
18. Chemical leaks	49. Insider trading	80. Solicitation
19. Child abuse	50. Intolerance	81. Televangelists
20. Conservatism	51. Junk bonds	82. Terrorism
21. Corruption	52. Junk food	83. Torture
22. Deforestation	53. Land fills	84. Toxic waste
23. Discrimination	54. Larceny	85. TV dinners
24. Dishonesty	55. Loitering	86. Tyranny
25. Drug addiction	56. Loss of laughter	87. Vagrancy
26. Drug cartels	57. Money laundering	88. Vandalism
27. Embezzlement	58. Monopolies	89. Vegetarians
28. Extortion	59. Mugging	90. War
29. Famine	60. Murder	91. Xenophobia

Designer
Frédéric Metz
Design Firm & Client
Centre de Design de l'Universite
du Québec, Canada

Invitation series for openings

Designers
Melanie Bass, Claire Wolfman
Design Firm
Grafik Communications Ltd.,
Alexandria, Virginia
Illustrator
Melanie Bass
Client
National Museum of Natural
History, Smithsonian Institution

Designer/Illustrator
Seymour Chwast
Design Firm
The Pushpin Group Inc.,
New York
Client
Lustrare Gallery

Invitation

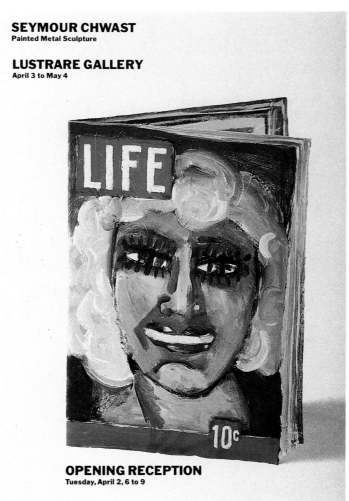

SEYMOUR CHWAST
Painted Metal Sculpture

LUSTRARE GALLERY
April 3 to May 4

OPENING RECEPTION
Tuesday, April 2, 6 to 9

Art Director/Designer
Takaaki Matsumoto
Design Firm
M Plus M Incorporated,
New York
Client
Gallery 91

Exhibition invitation/catalogue for
"Design Message from Japan"

Art Director/Designer
Peter Hollingsworth
Design Firm
Peter Hollingsworth &
Associates, Winston-Salem,
N. Carolina
Photographer
Merry Moor Winnett
Copywriter
Chris Yarborough
Client
Sawtooth Center for Visual
Design

*Chris Yarborough Artist of the
Year brochure*

Wylie,
my husband,
says I've kept
the child inside
me alive.
I say, when the
child inside dies,
so do you.

Creative/Art Director
Oscar Fernández
Designer
Gary Sankey
Design Firm & Client
Wexner Center for the Arts,
Columbus, Ohio
Copywriter
Sarah Rogers-Lafferty

Exhibition catalogue

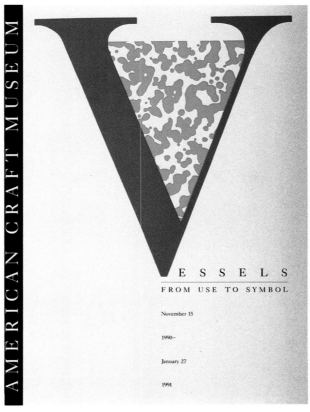

Designers
Joe Scorsone, Alice Drueding
Design Firm
Scorsone/Drueding, Jenkintown,
Pennsylvania
Copywriters
Nina Stritzler, John Perreault
Client
American Craft Museum,
New York City

Exhibition catalogue

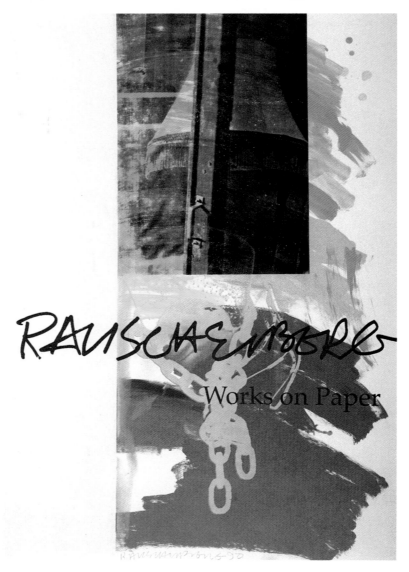

Creative/Art Directors
Meg Wilson, Greg Dittmar
Designer
Greg Dittmar
Design Firm & Client
Dallas Museum of Art, Texas
Photographers
Zindman/Fremont
Copywriter
Annegreth Nill

Brochure for exhibition series

Creative/Art Director
David Curry
Design Firm
David Curry Design, New York
Client
Knoedler & Company

Exhibition catalogue

Art Director/Designer
Julie Szamocki
Design Firm
Yamamoto Moss, Minneapolis,
Minnesota
Photographer
Gary Mortensen
Copywriters
Alastair Duncan, David Ryan
Client
Norwest Banks

Poster and brochure

Art Director/Designer
Greg Dittmar
Design Firm & Client
Dallas Museum of Art, Texas

Exhibition invitation

Designers
Ned Drew, Susan English,
Judy Kirpich
Design Firm
Grafik Communications Ltd.,
Alexandria, Virginia
Client
National Air & Space Museum

Report cover

The History of

SYMPOSIUM

Twentieth-Century

SATURDAY

American Craft:

NOVEMBER 17, 1990

A Centenary Project

A decade-long program of symposia, exhibitions, and catalogues organized by the American Craft Museum to write the history of twentieth-century American craft by the year 2000.

1900–1918:
The Foundation of the American Craft Movement
The first in a series of eight symposia on the history of twentieth-century American craft.

SYMPOSIUM PARTICIPANTS

Gary E. Baker, Curator, Glass
The Chrysler Museum

Eileen Boris, Associate Professor, History
Howard University

Leslie Bowman, Curator, Decorative Arts
Los Angeles County Museum of Art

W. Scott Braznell, Curator
American Silver Museum

Robert Judson Clark, Professor, Art and Archaeology
Princeton University

Martin Eidelberg, Professor, Art History
Rutgers University

Christa C. Mayer-Thurman, Curator, Textiles
The Art Institute of Chicago

Elizabeth Milroy, Assistant Professor, Art History
Wesleyan University

Kenneth R. Trapp, Curator, Crafts and Decorative Arts
The Oakland Museum

November 17, 1990
9:00–5:00

"The History of Twentieth-Century American Craft: A Centenary Project" is made possible in part by generous grants from the National Endowment for the Arts and The J. M. Kaplan Fund.

For further information, please contact:
Centenary Project Coordinator
American Craft Museum
40 West 53d Street
New York, New York 10019

Symposium Fee: $75
Members: $65

Patrons: $1,000 includes private dinner at a collector's home, November 17, invitation to observe the roundtable panel discussion by experts on Sunday, November 18, and tax-deductible contribution to "A Centenary Project" research.

To register for the symposium on November 17, 1990, enclose a check for $75 ($65 for American Craft Museum and Council members).

To register for the symposium and become a member of the American Craft Museum, enclose a check for $115 (Membership: Individual $50, Dual $65).

To register for the series (eight symposia over two years; schedule to be announced), enclose a check for $540 ($468 for American Craft Museum and Council members).

To register as a Patron, enclose $1,000 (Series Patron: $7,000).

The History of
Twentieth-Century
American Craft:
A Centenary Project

☐ I am currently a Museum or Council member.

American Craft Museum
40 West 53d Street
New York, New York 10019

Enclosed is a check payable to the American Craft Museum for $ _____

Account # ☐ American Express ☐ VISA ☐ MasterCard

Signature _____ Expiration date _____

Name _____

Organization _____

Address _____

City _____ State _____ Zip _____

Daytime telephone _____

Art Director
Leslee Avchen
Designers
Leslee Avchen, Laurie Jacobi
Design Firm
Avchen and Associates Inc.,
Minneapolis, Minnesota
Photographers
Judy Olausen, Rick Bell
Copywriter
Caroline Hall Otis
Client
The Science Museum of Minnesota

Campaign brochure

THE CAMPAIGN FOR
THE SCIENCE MUSEUM
OF MINNESOTA

Designers
Joe Scorsone, Alice Drueding
Design Firm
Scorsone/Drueding, Jenkintown,
Pennsylvania
Copywriter
Linda Craighead
Client
American Craft Museum,
New York City

Announcement/registration for symposium on 20th century crafts

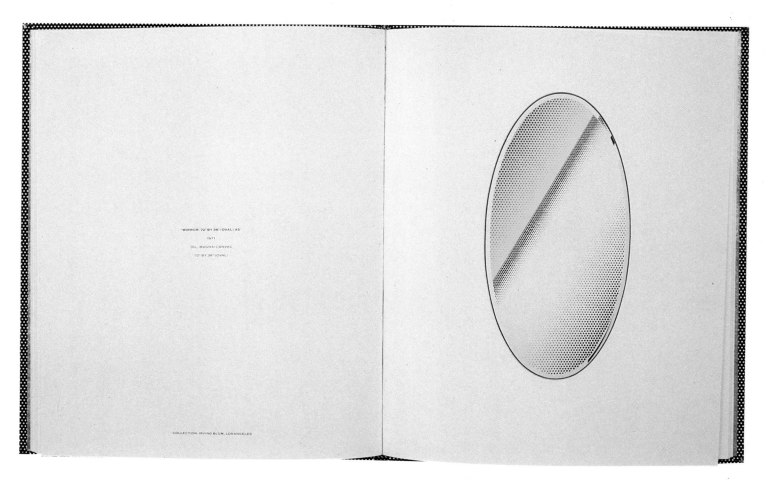

Art Director
Anthony McCall
Designer
John Bernstein
Design Firm
Anthony McCall Associates,
New York
Client
Mary Boone Gallery

*Roy Lichtenstein exhibition
catalogue*

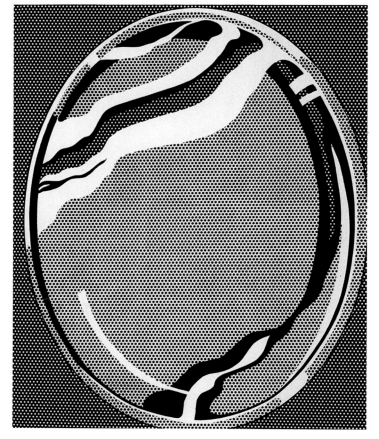

BREAKTHROUGHS

Avant-Garde Artists in Europe and America, 1950–1990

Art Director
Oscar Fernández
Designer
Alan Jazak
Design Firm & Client
Wexner Center Design for the
Arts, Columbus, Ohio

Tadashi Kawamata

Robert Stearns A few years ago in another interview, you said you were first interested in painting and then focused on the structure of the painting.

Tadashi Kawamata My initial interest was in the physical construction of the canvas. The structures of the painting, the wooden material of the stretcher bars, seemed more interesting than the flat surface of the painting. This was a point of departure, of exploration. But even more, I found it interesting to consider the painting within the space of the studio. It wasn't just the painting itself and the physical construction of the painting that intrigued me but also the painting as a physical object within the space.

As I continued this exploration, I became interested in constructing space. I found that if you put a large enough canvas on the wall, the distinction between the wall and the canvas disappears—the canvas becomes the wall. If you put the canvas on the floor, it becomes the floor.

RS So, for you, the work itself cannot be separated from the site or surrounding space?

TK Yes, it is individual. I take my material from the particular space and the problems that particular space presents to me.

RS You have stated that you don't create to exhibit but rather exhibit to create—that you begin the creative planning once an exhibition has been arranged.

TK I begin with the "order" when you put in your order for an exhibition. Before that I have absolutely nothing in my mind—it's absolutely blank until I am presented with the order, and then I fill that order. I am using the double meaning of "order" something that you demand from somebody as well as the arrangement of elements that meets a certain demand.

RS For you, are different spaces easier or harder to work with?

TK Again, I wait for the request. Then I begin to focus, though not immediately on the specific work that I'm going to produce. I begin to consider the space itself and its requirements, its utility, the kinds of people who are going to come to it, the positioning of the building and the space it occupies. In other words, I begin with a general concept, the situation, the sociological condition of the place and its relationship with the audience and me, the artist.

RS Several of your works—the project for the Japanese Pavilion at the Venice Biennale in 1982 and Destroyed Church in Kassel at Documenta in 1987—have been expressively extroverted, appearing to explode outward from public structures. Others—the project at the Takara House apartment in Tokyo in 1982—have been located in private, interior spaces not traditionally used for art. Are you interested in continuing to explore these two very different kinds of space?

TK Some places have a great historical significance; others are neutral. They have no special presence or history. In my earlier works, I used neutral spaces and was very much interested in them. The Takara House project was one example and By-Land (1979) was another. At that time, I was more interested in the conditions of the particular location than in any historical connections.

When I was first working in Tokyo, in the neutral spaces, the materials themselves didn't have much meaning. When I worked inside a house that was made of wood, there wasn't much difference between that wood and the wood I was using in my own projects. The first thing I confronted when I went to Europe was the use of very different building materials, stone and so on. The Biennale and Documenta gave me an opportunity to work in a historical setting, where the structures had significant social activity in there before I was there.

215   217

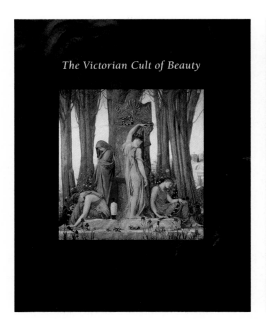

Art Director/Designer
Marilyn Bouma-Pyper
Design Firm & Client
Art Gallery of Ontario, Canada
Illustrator
William Black Richmond
Copywriter
Nancy Minty

*Catalogue for exhibit on the
Victorian Cult of Beauty*

Creative/Art Director
John Bernstein
Designer
Carrie Berman
Design Firm
Anthony McCall Associates,
New York
Client
Vrej Baghoomian Gallery

Kahlil Gibran exhibition catalogue

Art Director
John Bernstein
Design Firm
Anthony McCall Associates,
New York
Client
The Quillan Company

*The Quillan Collection of 19th
and 20th century photographs.*

Art Director/Designer
Gretchen Frederick
Design Firm
Invisions Ltd., Washington, D.C.
Copywriter
Elizabeth Weil
Client
National Gallery of Art

Publication of corporate displays

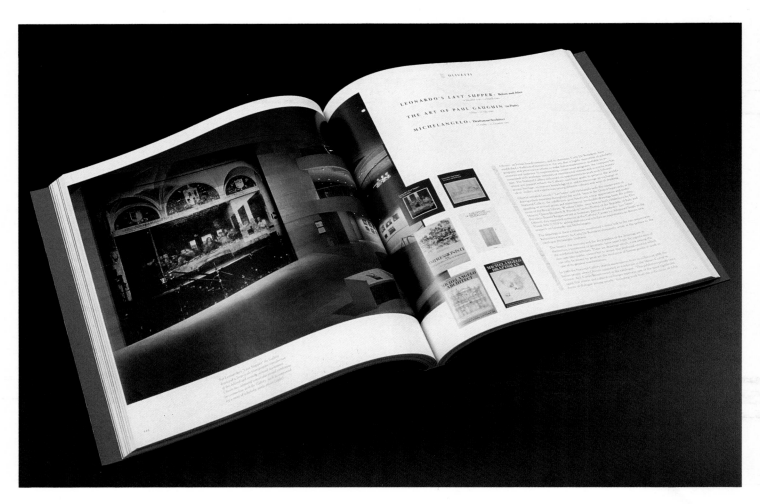

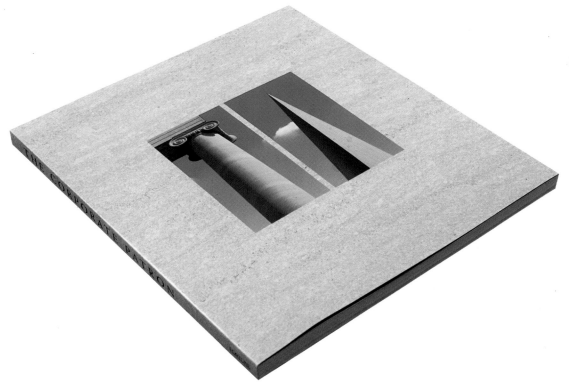

Creative/Art Directors
David Kusin, Greg Dittmar
Designer
Greg Dittmar
Design Firm & Client
Dallas Museum of Art, Texas
Photographer
Tom Jenkins
Copywriter
Dr. Anne Bromberg

Exhibition catalogue

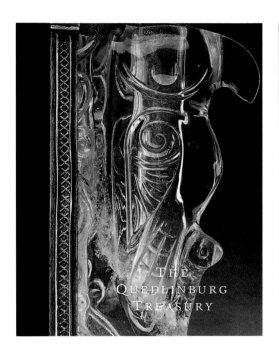

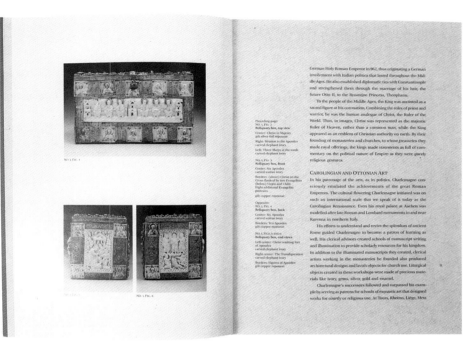

Designer
David Curry
Design Firm
David Curry Design, New York
Client
Knoedler & Company

Exhibition catalogue

Art Director
Anthony McCall
Designer
John Bernstein
Design Firm
Anthony McCall Associates,
New York
Client
Mary Boone Gallery

*Barbara Kruger exhibition
catalogue*

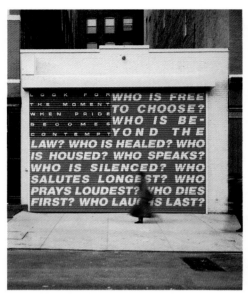

Busy killing Busy robbing Busy blaming Busy praying Busy preaching Busy fearing Busy hating Busy going crazy Busy boasting Busy raping Busy dying for your country Busy counting money Busy losing money Busy competing Busy judging Busy being correct Busy dividing and conquering Busy making history Busy bonding Busy wanting Busy putting women in their place Busy humiliating Busy strategizing Busy avoiding empathy Busy killing Busy robbing Busy blaming Busy praying Busy preaching Busy fearing Busy hating Busy going crazy Busy boasting Busy raping Busy dying for your country Busy counting money Busy losing money Busy competing Busy judging Busy being correct Busy dividing and conquering Busy making history Busy bonding Busy wanting Busy putting women in their place Busy humiliating Busy strategizing Busy avoiding empathy Busy killing Busy robbing Busy blaming Busy praying Busy preaching Busy fearing Busy hating Busy going crazy Busy boasting Busy raping Busy dying for your country Busy counting money Busy losing money Busy competing Busy judging Busy being correct Busy dividing and conquering Busy making history Busy bonding Busy wanting Busy putting women in their place Busy humiliating Busy strategizing Busy avoiding empathy Busy killing Busy robbing Busy blaming Busy praying Busy preaching Busy fearing Busy hating Busy going crazy Busy boasting Busy raping Busy dying for your country Busy counting money Busy losing money Busy competing Busy judging Busy being correct Busy dividing and conquering Busy making history Busy bonding Busy wanting Busy putting women in their place Busy humiliating Busy strategizing Busy avoiding empathy Busy killing Busy robbing Busy blaming Busy praying Busy preaching Busy fearing Busy hating Busy going crazy Busy boasting Busy raping Busy dying for your country Busy counting money Busy losing money Busy competing Busy judging Busy being correct Busy dividing and conquering Busy making history Busy bonding Busy wanting Busy putting women in their place Busy humiliating Busy strategizing Busy avoiding empathy Busy killing Busy robbing Busy blaming Busy praying Busy preaching Busy fearing Busy

The vomiting body screams "Kiss me" to the shitting body which coos "Smell me" to the vain body which hisses "I want you inside of me" to the dead body which is hard to dispose of.

Susan Dallas-Swann

Richard Harned

expansions 1

Expansions 1
26 January through 24 February 1991
Wexner Center for the Arts
The Ohio State University

Susan Dallas-Swann

Susan Dallas-Swann was born in Nashville, Tennessee and raised in northern Texas. She received a BS in Education from North Texas State and pursued studies at the School of the Art Institute, Chicago, IL. She has taught at Wake Forest University and The North Carolina School of the Arts, Winston-Salem, and the University of Massachusetts, Amherst, MA. Dallas-Swann currently lives and works in Columbus and New York City. She is an Associate Professor in the Department of Art's Expanded Arts Program at The Ohio State University.

In the mid-1970s, Dallas-Swann began using light and technology in her artwork. She worked with both standard lighting equipment and her own specially-designed light machines. Earlier works included light performances in which Dallas-Swann designed paintings and interactive light sculpture.

Susan Dallas-Swann began creating installations in the 1980s including a project at Grand Central Station, New York City and another in the rail station in Stamford, Connecticut, on the Hartford line connecting New York City and Boston.

Her recent work includes a ten year project conceived during a residency at the Headlands Center for the Arts, Sausalito, California based on the vernal equinox. Each year, for the remainder of the century, Dallas-Swann hopes to expand the exploration of the socio-political importance of the natural light effects of the equinox.

She has received grants from the National Endowment for the Arts, the New York Council for the Arts, the Ohio Arts Council, and The Ohio State University's Small Research Grants Program.

Richard Harned

Richard Harned was born in New Haven, Connecticut in 1953. He received his BFA in sculpture and MFA in glass at the Rhode Island School of Design, where he studied with Dale Chihuly, who is internationally renowned for his work in glass. Harned taught courses in glass and sculpture at the Pilchuck in Stanwood, WA, the Rhode Island School of Design, and the Arkansas State University in Jonesboro. Presently, Harned lives and works in Columbus and is an Associate Professor in the Department of Art at The Ohio State University, where he directs the glass arts program.

After his studies, Harned began to explore non-traditional uses of glass as material for sculpture and installation. His large-scale installations incorporate neon, movement, and, most recently, telecommunications systems.

Harned has exhibited throughout the United States and in Paris, France. Recently, he participated in the Glassworks exhibition at the Renwick Gallery, Smithsonian Institute, Washington, D.C.

He has received Individual Fellowship Grants in Sculpture from the NEA and the Greater Columbus Arts Council, as well as Grant and University Small Research Grants from The Ohio State University.

Art Director
Oscar Fernández
Designer
Gary Sankey
Design Firm & Client
Wexner Center for the Arts,
Columbus, Ohio
Copywriter
Sarah Rogers-Lafferty

Exhibition catalogue

Art Director/Designer
Félix Beltrán
Design Firm
Félix Beltrán & Asociados,
Mexico
Client
Galería Tigra, Mexico

Hard Edge exhibition catalogue

Creative/Art Directors
Mark Sylvester, Lisa Taft
Design Firm
Cranbrook Academy of Art,
Bloomfield Hills, Michigan
Copywriter
Gerry Craig
Client
Detroit Artist Market

Calendar

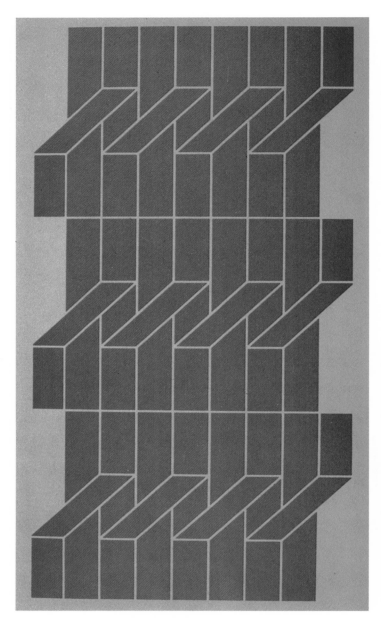

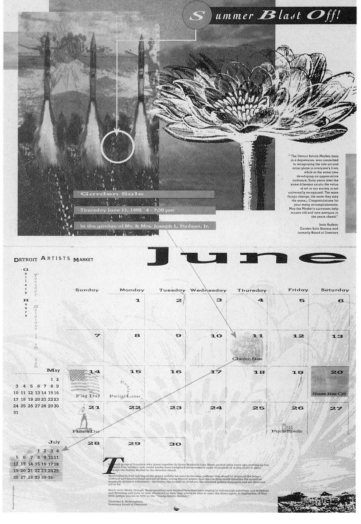

to cast it in tubes, allow them to set, then cut and spin them on a lathe to produce decorative knobs and handles.

Before World War II, plastics were considered modern and fascinating materials. They were used for adult goods and luxury items. With World War II, the industry focused on America's war effort, and the plastic goods produced were often shoddy and inferior. By the end of the war, consumers saw plastics as cheap and undesirable. This image has only slowly receded.

In spite of the negative image post-war plastics possessed, the industry rapidly developed new materials. Among these were melamine, used for tableware, PVC, nylon, acrylic, polystyrene, and polyethylene, used for hula hoops and Tupperware. These last two materials were petrochemical plastics based on coal tar gas. They could be dyed bright colors, were rigid, easily produced, and had a low production cost. They were generally molded, most often injection molded. Because of these factors, they were popular choices for post-war child appeal premiums.

There are few facets of modern life that plastics do not influence. In 1982 the plastics industry outproduced the steel industry worldwide, and a long-predicted Plastics Age arrived. Plastics are utilitarian, yet designers can employ them in luxury furniture and jewelry items. Their miraculous ability to meet modern needs is almost overlooked because of their ubiquity. From their early invention to the present, consumer and manufacturer interest and dependence on plastics have steadily grown, until they are now a necessary part of modern life.

G.G.

1. *The Oxford English Dictionary, Vol. VII Oxford: The Clarendon Press, 1933; p. 959.*
2. *Scientific American, Vol. 174, No. 4, April 1946, pp. 158-160.*

INTERVIEW

This interview with John Charles (Wally) Walworth Jr. took place in April of this year.

Q What can you tell us about your early family life?

A I was born on September 7, 1913 in New Rochelle, New York. My parents, John Charles Walworth and Jessie Viola

Mosher were native New Yorkers who had been introduced to each other on a tennis court in Central Park. They married in 1895 and I was the last of their four sons. The oldest, Chester, was born in 1898 and the siblings followed, spaced either purposely or by accident, four or five years apart. In 1902 Mead was born, followed by Frederick in 1906, and I arrived

five years later.

As the family story goes, my father didn't relish the idea of naming any of my brothers after himself. But by the time I came along, my mother's sister, actress Mabel Montgomery, threatened to hit my father over the head with a bottle of champagne if he didn't "name this one Junior." Typically, we were all nicknamed "Wally."

When I was seven, the family moved from New Rochelle back into the city because my father had inherited the Walworth Business School from his father. It was located on the Walworth Building on Walworth Square at 149th Street and Melrose Avenue in the Bronx. It was one of three schools which taught stenography and typing. The others were in Manhattan on 125th Street, and there was one on Columbus Circle.

Q Did you have creative or artistic tendencies as a child? Did it run in the family?

A From my earliest childhood I enjoyed drawing, but most of my influences came from outside the family. Though my father and grandfather drew a little bit, and my brother Fred had technical drafting skills, I was really the only one in my family with any artistic inclination. I would lie on the living room floor and copy the comic strips and cartoons from newspapers and magazines like *Life* and *College Humor*. My daughter Joan inherited her interest in art from me.

Q When did others notice you had a fondness for art, and for caricature in particular?

Art Director/Designer
Martha Carothers
Design Firm
The Post Press, Newark, Delaware
Illustrators/Photographers
John Walworth, Kathleen Clark, Peter Croydon, Raymond Nichols, Bob Herbert
Copywriter
Belena Chapp
Client
University Gallery, University of Delaware

Exhibition brochure

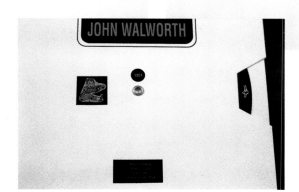

Art Director
Anthony McCall
Designers
Donald Burg, John Bernstein
Design Firm
Anthony McCall Associates, New York
Client
Hirschl & Adler Modern

Series of exhibition catalogues

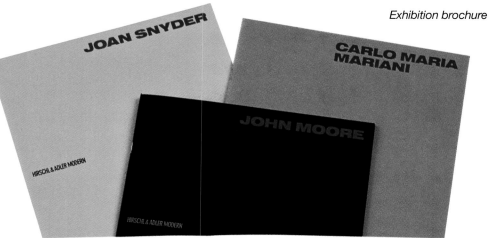

12
13

Art Director
Joyce Nesnadny
Designers
Joyce Nesnadny, Ruth D'Emilia
Design Firm
Nesnadny & Schwartz,
Cleveland, Ohio
Copywriter
Wendy Kendall-Hess
Client
Akron Art Museum

Brochure

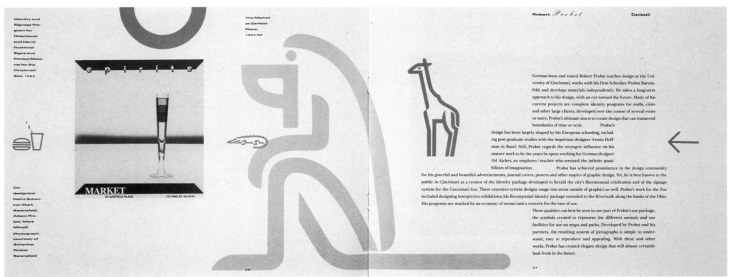

Art Director/Designer
Ann Wassmann Gross
Design Firm & Client
The Art Institute of Chicago
Copywriter
Valjean McLenighan

Fund-raising booklet

Art Director
Oscar Fernández
Designer
Gary Sankey
Design Firm & Client
Wexner Center for the Arts,
Columbus, Ohio
Copywriter
Elizabeth Krouse

Season newsletters

Art Director
Oscar Fernández
Designers
Oscar Fernández, M.
Christopher Jones, Gary Sankey
Design Firm & Client
Wexner Center for the Arts,
Columbus, Ohio
Copywriters
Elizabeth Krouse, Patricia
Trumps, Jonathan Green

Brochures

Exhibition catalogue

Art Director/Designer
Katharine Douglass
Design Firm&Client
North Carolina Museum of Art,
Raleigh
Photographer
British Museum
Copywriter
Patrick McCusker

*Invitation for gala opening of
British watercolours exhibition*

Creative Director
Stephen Archibald
Designer
David Carter
Design Firm & Client
Nova Scotia Museum, Canada
Photographer
Ron Merrick
Copywriters
Ruth Whitehead, Joleen Gordon

*Information sheet promoting
exhibition – produced in
celebration of The Year of
Basketry, 1991.*

Art Directors/Designers
Walter McCord, Julius Friedman
Design Firm
CHOPLOGIC, Louisville,
Kentucky
Illustrator
Walter McCord
Client
Portland Museum, Louisville

Stationery

Art Director
Chris Spivey
Designers
Chris Spivey (business papers)
Tim Girvin (identity)
Design Firm
Tim Girvin Design Inc., Seattle,
Washington
Client
Sandra Collins Gallery

*Stationery for a gallery of original
artist's works*

Art Director/Designer
Jack Anderson
Designer
Carole Jones
Design Firm
Hornall Anderson Design Works,
Seattle, Washington
Illustrator
Jack Anderson
Client
Howard/Mandville Gallery

Stationery

"MOST PEOPLE THINK OF RAINBOWS AS RANDOM ACTS OF NATURE. TO SCULPTOR DALE ELDRED, THEY'RE THE RAW MATERIALS FOR HIS ART." — NEWSWEEK

JUSTYNE FISCHER, FRESHMAN FOUNDATION STUDENT, KALAMAZOO, MICHIGAN

"VANDERBYL IS RESPONSIBLE FOR MORE SUPERB CORPORATE LOGOS THAN ANY OTHER DESIGNER OF HIS GENERATION." — TIME

MICHAEL VANDERBYL, JOYCE C. HALL DISTINGUISHED PROFESSOR OF DESIGN, 1988-1989

"HERE, YOU HAVE TO CHALLENGE YOURSELF ... YOU DON'T GET ANY HANDOUTS. YOU'RE EXPECTED TO THINK FOR YOURSELF, WORK BY YOURSELF, AND DEVELOP YOUR OWN OPINIONS."

"THE LATEST WORK OF KEN FERGUSON, A CERAMIST, EXHALES ENERGY — PSYCHIC, KINETIC, EROTIC AND MYTHIC." — THE NEW YORK TIMES

Creative/Art Directors
Jane Weeks, John Muller
Design Firm
Muller & Co., Kansas City, Missouri
Photographer
John Krueger
Client
Kansas City Art Institute

Brochure

KANSAS CITY ART INSTITUTE

Art Director/Designer
Marilyn Bouma-Pypęr
Design Firm & Client
Art Gallery of Ontario, Canada
Photographers
Carlos Catenazzi, Clive Webster
Copywriter
Marilyn Litvak

Booklet was designed to highlight the Grange House, one of the oldest brick houses in Toronto and also the Art Gallery of Ontario's first home.

Art Director/Designer
William J. Kolano
Design Firm
Irene Pasinski Associates Inc.,
Pittsburgh, Pennsylvania
Client
Pittsburgh Fund for Arts
Education

Exhibition catalogue

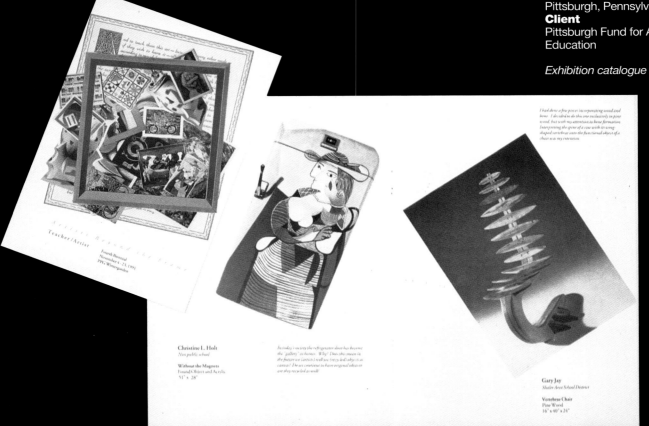

Art Director
Anthony McCall
Designer
Wing Chan
Design Firm
Anthony McCall Associates,
New York
Client
Barbara Gladstone Gallery

Announcement cards

Designer
David Curry
Design Firm
David Curry Design, New York
Client
Art In America

Cover for annual guide

Art Direct
Takaaki Mat
Design Fir
M Plus M In
New York
Client
Metropolitar

Multi-lingua

Creative/A
Jane Weeks
Design Fir
Muller & Co
Missouri
Client
Kansas City

Exhibition c

75 MILLION YEARS OF ART AND OBJECTS
Part Two

MEMPHITE AXE
CHINA, 2ND MILLENNIUM B.C.

VOTIVE RELIEF OF CLEOPATRA
EGYPT, 2ND CENTURY B.C.

SUKOTHAI BUDDHA
THAILAND, 14TH-15TH CENTURY

LIMOGES BRONZE CLASP
FRANCE, 12TH CENTURY

Art Director
John Bernstein
Design Firm
Anthony McCall Associates,
New York
Client
Anthony Ralph Gallery

*Announcement card for 75
million years of art and objects*

Creative/Art Directors
John Muller, Scott Chapman
Design Firm
Muller & Co., Kansas City,
Missouri
Client
Kansas City Art Institute

Magazine

ASSEMBLAGE
KANSAS CITY ART INSTITUTE MAGAZINE
FALL 1991

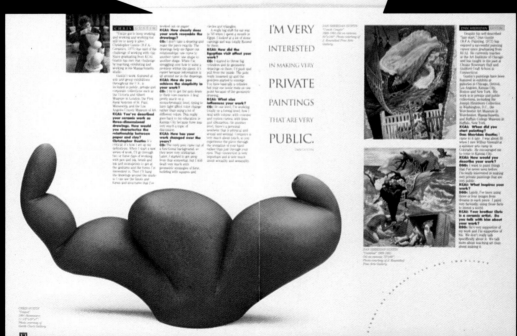

I'M VERY
INTERESTED
IN MAKING VERY
PRIVATE
PAINTINGS
THAT ARE VERY
PUBLIC.

Art Director/Designer
Steven Joseph
Design Firm
Spatchurst Design Associates,
N.S.W., Australia
Client
Art Gallery of New South Wales

*Information and programme
bulletin produced every second
month for the art gallery*

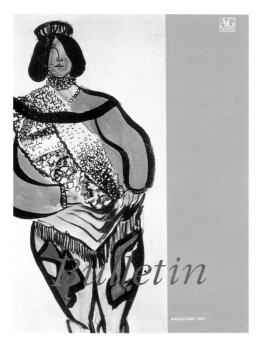

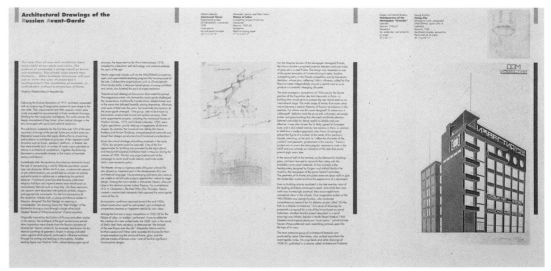

Designer
Oscar Fernández
Design Firm & Client
Wexner Center for the Arts.,
Columbus, Ohio
Copywriter
Emily Kies Folpe

Brochure

Art Director
Oscar Fernández
Designer
Gary Sankey
Design Firm & Client
Wexner Center for the Arts,
Columbus, Ohio
Copywriter
Elizabeth Krouse

Event brochure

a special evening

Media Arts

The fact that one of the Wexner Center's three programming departments should operate under the rubric of "Media Arts" testifies to the increased centrality within contemporary culture of the moving image. Drawing on traditions begun in the 19th century with the invention of the cinema and extending into the present with independent artists working in film, video, and affiliated forms, the Media Arts program is responsible for presenting public screenings from two to three evenings per week of challenging works in virtually all genres and formats.

Between January and December 1991, the Media Arts program will have presented over 160 individual works. Selections highlighting various national cinemas include: *Romanian Film Off the Shelf; Projected Radiance—The Cinema of Indonesia; The Banned and the Beautiful—Czech and Slovak Filmmaking, 1963-1971; South American Scenes; Swiss Classics, 1923-1945; French Lessons;* and *Perspective Canada.* Works produced by and addressing concerns of women and people of color include: *Women's Work; Prized Pieces Award Winners,* as well as series presented in conjunction with Asian-American Awareness and Hispanic Awareness Weeks, and gay-lesbian communities. Other series tackling social issues include *New Advocacies I and II,* and *Wastelands.* Series focusing on particular individuals such as Yoko Ono, Keith Carradine, Twyla Tharp, and Harold Pinter were also screened.

The Media Arts program has hosted area premieres of a number of adventurous foreign and domestic feature films such as: *Poison; The Ballad of the Sad Cafe; Route One; The Garden; Young Soul Rebels; Salmonberries; Swan Lake—The Zone,* among others. In addition, the Media Arts program has hosted nine Visiting Artists who introduced and discussed their work with the audience. These include Jim McKay, Tom Hayes, Peggy Ahwesh, David Peck, Roddy Bogawa, Twyla Tharp, Reno Dakota, Peter Watkins, and Isaac Julien. In conjunction with the *Passages de l'image* exhibition, Media Arts presented an accompanying film series, as well as a seven-part video series of over two dozen tapes on view throughout the duration of the exhibition.

Parallel to this commitment to presentation is a commitment to assist artists in the creation of new work. Presently, members of the New York-based media collective, Paper Tiger Television are in residence for the creation of the installation, *Dream House,* as well as for the production of three new tapes. In residence during the past summer was veteran film/video artist Mark Rappaport, who used the Center's technical resources to complete pre-production for two new works.

The Media Arts program's second major area of responsibility is the Wexner Center's Art & Technology facility — a video and film production and post-production studio with cameras, graphic and on-line editing equipment. The sophistication of this facility is such as to render the Wexner Center as the only fully integrated arts center in this country able to provide full on-site support for the production of new media works, and is intended for use by artists working on projects at the Center.

Photographer Bruce Weber's Oscar nominated *Let's Get Lost*

Visiting artist Trin T. Minh-ha discussed her film *Surname Viet Given Name Nam*

19

WEXNER CENTER FOR THE ARTS
THE OHIO STATE UNIVERSITY

PASSAGES
de L'IMAGE

JUNE 1–OCTOBER 6, 1991

PASSAGES DE L'IMAGE

Since the invention of photography in the nineteenth century, artists and audiences alike have confronted the many issues raised by the ability of the camera to capture a "mechanical reproduction" (in philosopher Walter Benjamin's well-known phrase) of the world. Photography challenged traditional definitions of art objects as unique and handmade by introducing multiple, identical "originals" and interjecting a mechanical tool between the artist's hand and the finished artwork. Subsequently, each newly invented method of recording or creating images has raised additional questions regarding the nature of art and of representation.

The international exhibition *Passages de l'image* brings this investigation up to the present by exploring contemporary intersections and exchanges among photography, film, and video: art forms derived from mechanical reproduction. Christine Van Assche, Catherine David, and Raymond Bellour, the show's three organizers, selected works by fifteen artists—from Australia, Canada, France, Germany, and the United States—who use or combine these varied image-making techniques in provocative and innovative ways. The exhibited works include black-and-white and color photographic prints and projections, holograms, video installations, and multimedia installations that employ combinations of photographs, videos, films, computer images, and audio elements. All of the works date from the 1980s and 1990s; several were created for this show.

Mutual influences between photography and cinema, and between these media and painting or sculpture, have received much critical attention in recent years. *Passages de l'image* builds on these discussions with heightened considerations of video and of the newer techniques of computer image making. The exhibition title, which might be translated as "transitions of the image," refers to the continuing changes or shifts in the means by which images can be produced, recorded, presented, and interpreted. The phrase also suggests the interlaced connections between the various media represented in the show.

The works in the exhibition often involve aspects of more than one discipline or use the techniques of one medium to explore characteristics of another. Although still images are usually associated with photography and moving images with film and video, many of the artists represented here undermine these expectations, suggesting movement in photographic images or interjecting static elements into the moving-picture formats of film and video. Other artists investigate contradictory impulses toward documentary resemblance and theatrical fiction, both conventions with long traditions in photography, film, and video. Relationships among art, popular entertainment, and mass media also are recurrent themes in *Passages de l'image.*

The language of human poses, gestures, and facial expressions intrigues many artists in the show. To the exhibition's organizers this shared fascination with the body suggests a "humanizing" trend in contemporary art and particularly in video and the other art forms showcased in *Passages de l'image.* The emphasis on the body may reflect artists' efforts to counteract the "dehumanizing" tendencies sometimes associated with technologically complex media.

In addition to the artists' projects, *Passages de l'image* includes a group of computer images selected and presented by Professor Jean Louis Boissier of the University of Paris. Screenings of historical and contemporary films and videotapes related to the themes of the exhibition also are part of the Wexner Center's presentation of *Passages de l'image.*

Jeff Wall
Eviction Struggle
1988-89
Collection, Ydessa
Hendeles Foundation,
Toronto

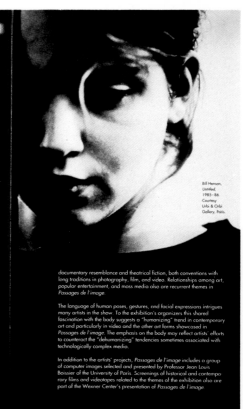

Bill Henson,
Untitled,
1985-86
Courtesy
Urbi & Orbi
Gallery, Paris.

Exhibition catalogue

Creative/Art Director
Oscar Fernández
Designer
Alan Jazak
Design Firm & Client
Wexner Center for the Arts.,
Columbus, Ohio
Copywriter
Ann Bremner

195

Art Director/Designer
Greg Dittmar
Design Firm & Client
Dallas Museum of Art, Texas
Illustrator
Greg Dittmar

Press kit, letterhead, brochure and binder for an exhibition

DMASEPTEMBER

1 EXHIBITION OPENS. *Designs for the Division Chairs from the Permanent Collection, North Carolina.*

2:00 p.m. FILMS. *Scent of Mystery, Sunrise; The Lady of the Frozen Sea.*

4 12:15 p.m. GALLERY TALK. *The Scene I'm In, Texas Art in the 1980's: Annegrete Neff.*

12:15 p.m. ARCHITECTURAL WALKING TOUR.

5 12:15 p.m. SPECIAL INTEREST TOUR. *Eugene Grivas, Ballet for Hope?*

6 7:30 p.m. PERFORMANCE. *El Pueblo Baca Concerto.*

7 7:30 p.m. PERFORMANCE. *El Pueblo Baca Concerto.*

8 1:00 p.m. ARTIST DEMONSTRATION

2:00 p.m. FILMS. *Joe's Bed-Stuy Barbershop, We Cut Heads; Illusions; Bless Their Little Hearts: A Film for Nappy-Headed People.*

Terry Allen.

11 12:15 p.m. GALLERY TALK. *Teachers and Influences: David Bates.*

12:15 p.m. ARCHITECTURAL WALKING TOUR.

7:30 p.m. CONCERT. Terry Allen.

12 12:15 p.m. SPECIAL INTEREST TOUR. *The Painter and the Victorian.*

7:30 p.m. CONCERT. *Frieta Link: The Devil Made Me Do It.*

13 EXHIBITION OPENS. *Suzanne Stearns, Carved Asian Jades, Decorative Arts Wing.*

14 1:00 p.m. CONCERT. *New Tradition.*

15 2:00 p.m. FILMS. *Seeking Two Masters; Down with Malindi.*

17 12:00 p.m. BROWN BAG LECTURE. *Rituals of the World by Constantine Brancusi.*

18 12:15 p.m. GALLERY TALK. *Otis Dozier, Henry Delahunt.*

12:15 p.m. ARCHITECTURAL WALKING TOUR.

19 12:15 p.m. SPECIAL INTEREST TOUR. *The Davies Ensemble, Art.*

7:00 p.m. LECTURE. *Paintings from the Maria Underwater Buying Exploration in Saq Square Court, Dr. Andrea Serra.*

20 2:00 p.m. PERFORMANCE. *El Diez y Seis.*

21 2:00 p.m. PERFORMANCE. *Celebrando El Diez y Seis.*

22 2:00 p.m. FILMS. *The Blood of Jesus, Picking Tribes; Cross.*

6:00 p.m. FILM. *The Comedian Harmonists.*

25 12:15 p.m. GALLERY TALK. *A Historian's Perspective on Dallas Artists in the Thirties, Michael V. Hazel.*

12:15 p.m. ARCHITECTURAL WALKING TOUR.

26 12:15 p.m. SPECIAL INTEREST TOUR. *The Pre-Columbian World.*

28 7:30 p.m. The V...

This Stage I'm In.

29 2:00 p.m. ARCHITECTURAL WALKING TOUR.

2:00 p.m. CONCERT. Lara Lovelse.

New Tradition's new painting.

Down with Malindi.

DMAOCTOBER

Architectural Walking Tour.

CONVERSATIONS
Jeffery Siegel

2 12:15 p.m. GALLERY TALK. *Designs for the Division Chairs, Texas.*

3 12:15 p.m. SPECIAL INTEREST TOUR. *The Scene I'm In, Texas Art in the 1980's.*

7:30 p.m. LECTURE. *Art for the Eternal World: Ancient Egyptian Tomb Paintings, Dr. Betsy Scott.*

6 2:00 p.m. FILM. *The Lady Eve.*

7 2:00 p.m. CONCERT. *The Splendor of Schubert.*

9 12:15 p.m. GALLERY TALK. *Picture of an Orderly World, Molly Green.*

10 12:15 p.m. SPECIAL INTEREST TOUR. *Artist as a Rebel.*

12 1:00 p.m. DROP-IN ART

2:00 p.m. CONCERT. Joseph Hagedorn

13 1:00 p.m. ARTIST DEMONSTRATION

2:00 p.m. FILM. *The Bitter Tea of General Yen.*

15 12:00 p.m. BROWN BAG LECTURE. *Face to Mask: Prints by Artists in Multiplications.*

16 12:15 p.m. GALLERY TALK. *A Full Fiesta!: The Day of the Dead, Stephen Villarin.*

7:30 p.m. LECTURE. *Octavio and the Golden Age of French Porcelain, Rosalind Savill.*

17 12:15 p.m. SPECIAL INTEREST TOUR. *Considering the Spiritual in Art.*

Christopher Adkins and Jo Boatwright.

19 2:00 p.m. CONCERT. *Brunellis Rendezvous on the Bluegrass, Christopher Adkins and Jo Boatwright.*

20 2:00 p.m. FILM. *African Film.*

23 12:15 p.m. GALLERY TALK. *Women Relationships: The Ties That Bind, Gail Davitt.*

24 12:15 p.m. SPECIAL INTEREST TOUR. *The Reves Collection: Living in the Past.*

7:00 p.m. LECTURE. *Skyscrapers of Ancient Mexico, Anthony Aveni.*

26 1:00 p.m. DROP-IN ART

Anthony Aveni.

27 12:15 p.m. ARCHITECTURAL WALKING TOUR.

2:00 p.m. FILM. *Bringing Up Baby.*

30 12:15 p.m. GALLERY TALK. *Beyond the Marks, Adam Haine.*

31 12:15 p.m. SPECIAL INTEREST TOUR. *The Paintings of Modern Life.*

Covered Vase, Sevres Factory, 1778, Porcelain, Inventory of Rosenberg and Neibel.

DMAGENDA

Dallas Museum of Art

November/December 1991

Volume 1, Number 2 $2.00

5   6

11

14   Acropolis Frieze

20   Acropolis Frieze

MARY (BEBE) & CROSBY KEMPER

"I just enjoy art and I want everybody else to enjoy it. I think that anybody who does well and is successful should give back to the community. My father and my uncle believed that."

"Now Bebe and I have assembled a permanent collection of contemporary art for the students and the people of the community to enjoy. We focused on contemporary art because that has not been accented in Kansas City."

"Kansas City Art Institute, as an educational institution, is involved in shaping students' tastes during the formative stages of their careers. I hope the students can become friends with the permanent collection — that it will open their minds and spirits to be in direct contact with that kind of greatness."
R. Crosby Kemper, Jr. January 1991.

"It's impossible to say which pieces are my favorites, because there are so many wonderful works. We've assembled the Collection with the educational value of the works foremost in our minds."
Bebe Kemper, January 1991.

R. Crosby Kemper, Jr. chairman and CEO of United Missouri Bancshares, Inc., grew up in a family of art patrons and has contributed generously to many civic and arts organizations in Kansas City. His wife Mary — better known by her nickname Bebe — Kemper, is a member of the Kansas City Institute Board of Trustees and is a practicing and exhibiting artist.

R. Crosby Kemper is the grandson of Mrs. Charlotte Crosby Kemper, who was instrumental in the early development of an exhibition program at Kansas City Art Institute. The establishment of the Charlotte Crosby Kemper Gallery at Kansas City Art Institute in 1963 was made possible through the gifts of Charlotte Crosby Kemper's sons, William T. Kemper, Jr. R. Crosby Kemper and James M. Kemper. Since its inception, the Charlotte Crosby Kemper Gallery has achieved a national reputation as a leader in contemporary visual art exhibitions and programming.

In early 1990, Mr. R. Crosby Kemper announced a generous gift to Kansas City Art Institute to establish the Kemper Museum of Contemporary Art and Design of Kansas City Art Institute. The Mary and Crosby Kemper Collection of Kansas City Art Institute will enhance the future Museum with a remarkable visual resource for the enrichment of Kansas City Art Institute students as well as the greater Kansas City community.

GEORGIA O'KEEFFE
"Autumn Trees — The Chestnut Tree — Red" 1924
Oil on canvas, 36¼" x 30"
Plate~1

Creative/Art Directors
Jane Weeks, John Muller
Design Firm
Muller & Co., Kansas City, Missouri
Client
Kansas City Art Institute

Exhibition catalogue

Creative/Art Directors
Takaaki Matsumoto, Michael
McGinn
Designer
Takaaki Matsumoto
Design Firm
M Plus M Incorporated,
New York
Client
Fashion Institute of Technology

Invitation

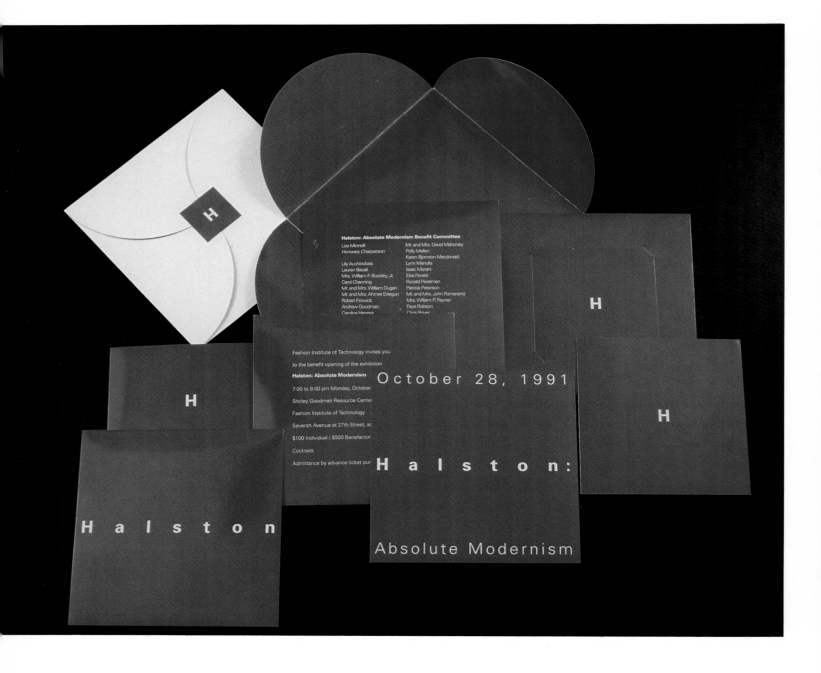

Creative/Art Directors
Michael McGinn, Takaaki Matsumoto
Designer
Michael McGinn
Design Firm
M Plus M Incorporated, New York
Client
Independent Curators Incorporated

Print material for the 15th anniversary benefit exhibition, silent auction and gala

Creative/Art Directors
Meg Wilson, Greg Dittmar
Designer
Greg Dittmar
Design Firm & Client
Dallas Museum of Art, Texas
Illustrator
Greg Dittmar

Invitation for ground-breaking ceremony of new museum wing

Designers
Melanie Bass, Judy Kirpich
Design Firm
Grafik Communications Ltd.,
Alexandria, Virginia
Illustrators
Enzo Messi, Urs Schmidt
Client
Smithsonian Institution Travelling
Exhibit Service

Design Director
Ivan Chermayeff
Designer
Anthony Williams
Design Firm
Chermayeff & Geismar Inc.,
New York
Client
Katonah Museum of Art

Design Director
Tom Geismar
Designer
Tom Geismar
Design Firm
Chermayeff & Geismar Inc.,
New York
Client
Museum of Modern Art

50th anniversary paper bag

Design Director
Ivan Chermayeff
Designer
Bill Anton
Design Firm
Chermayeff & Geismar Inc.,
New York
Client
Minneapolis College of Art and
Design

Art Director/Designer
Tony O'Hanlon
Design Firm
Red M, Galway, Ireland
Client
The Arts Council of Ireland

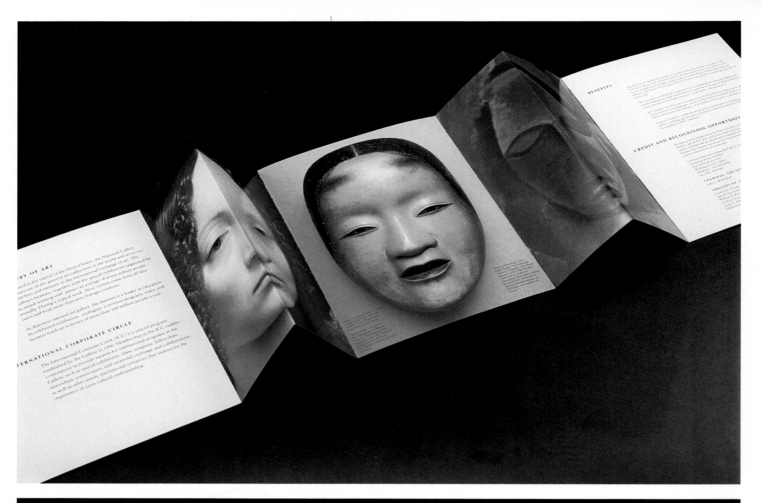

Brochure for corporate donations

Art Director
Gretchen Frederick
Design Firm
Invisions Ltd., Washington, D.C.
Copywriter
Elizabeth Weil
Client
National Gallery of Art

Art Director
John Hornall
Design Firm
Hornall Anderson Design Works
Designers
Mike Courtney, John Hornall,
Cliff Chung
Client
Seattle Art Museum

Construction barricade

Art Directors, Designers, Architects, Illustrators, Photographers, Copywriters, Fabricators